MODERN GREECE

A Partner or Still a Client?

George Kaloudis

University Press of America,® Inc.
Lanham · New York · Oxford

University Press of America,® Inc.
4720 Boston Way
Lanham, Maryland 20706

PO Box 317
Oxford
OX2 9RU, UK

Printed in the United States of America
British Library Cataloging in Publication Information Available

ISBN 0-7618-2419-7 (paperback : alk. ppr.)

™ The paper used in this publication meets the minimum requirements of American National Standard for Information Sciences—Permanence of Paper for Printed Library Materials, ANSI Z39.48—1984

Contents

Acknowledgments

I am thankful for support from many of my colleagues at Rivier College, especially Sr. Marjorie for expressing much interest about Greece. I owe many thanks to my family in Greece, to my children Stergos and Naomi for championing all of my projects, and to my wife, Penelope, for encouraging me to pursue my interests.

List of Abbreviations

ASPIDA	"Shield" (also an acronym for "Officers, Save Fatherland, Ideals, Democracy and Meritocracy")
EAM	National Liberation Front
EAN	Greek Anti-dictatorship Youth
EC	European Community
EDA	Union of the Democratic Left
EDES	National Republic Greek Army
EEC	European Economic Community
EENA	Union of Young Greek Officers
EK	Center Union
ELAS	National Liberation Army
EOKA	National Organization of Cypriot Combatants
ERE	National Radical Union
ERP	European Recovery Program of the Marshall Plan
ESA	Greek Military Police
EU	European Union
FIR	Flight Information Region
FYROM	Former Yugoslav Republic of Macedonia
ICAO	International Civil Aviation Organization
IDEA	Sacred League of Greek Officers
IMPs	Integrated Mediterranean Programs
KKE	Communist Party of Greece
KYP	Central Service of Information
NATO	North Atlantic Treaty Organization
ND	New Democracy
OTE	Greek Telecommunications Company
PAK	Panhellenic Liberation Movement
PASOK	Panhellenic Socialist Movement
UNFICYP	United Nations' Force in Cyprus

Introduction

The Treaty of Westphalia, which ended the Thirty Years' War (1618-1648), contained ten philosophical tenets: Retributive justice, assimilating losers into the postwar system, removing religion from international politics, state sovereignty, the equality of states, the balance of power, collective security and multilateral diplomacy, selective nonintervention, legitimizing *realpolitik*, and the demise of moral constraints (Kegley & Raymong, 2002, pp. 128-135). The treaty signified the beginning of modern international relations, encouraged the growth of international law, promoted the balance of power among European countries, and led to the establishment of an international system that is frequently described as the Westphalian order. According to Baylis and Smith (1997), this system was based on two primary principles: statehood and sovereignty.[1] Statehood meant that the world consisted of nation-states with strong centralized governments that had control in the area under their jurisdiction. In addition, the nation-state was sovereign, that is; it "exercised comprehensive, supreme, unqualified, and exclusive control over its designated territorial domain" (p. 20).

The nation-state continues to remain the dominant actor in the international system. But was nation-state sovereignty ever "comprehensive, supreme, unqualified, and exclusive"? Not all nation-states are created equal and the existence of power asymmetries among nation-states enables some of them to achieve greater degree of sovereignty than others. While great powers find it easier to protect their sovereignty, small and dependent powers are constantly confronted with the challenge of having their sovereignty compromised. Weak states often have to accept far greater interference from more powerful countries (Russett & Oneal, 2001, p. 18).

The term sovereignty has been used in four different ways: international legal sovereignty, Westphalian sovereignty, domestic sovereignty, and interdependence sovereignty. International legal sovereignty refers to the mutual recognition of states by other states; Westphalian sovereignty refers to the exclusion of external actors from domestic authority configurations; domestic sovereignty refers to the organization of public authority within a state and to the level of effective control exercised by those holding authority; and interdependence sovereignty refers to the ability of public authorities to control movements across territorial boundaries. International legal sovereignty and Westphalian sovereignty refer to issues of authority: that is, the recognition that the state has the authority to engage in international agreements and the right of a state to exclude external actors from its affairs. Domestic sovereignty refers to both authority and control: that is, the authority structures that are recognized within a state and the effectiveness of their control. Interdependence sovereignty refers to control: that is, the ability of a state to control movements across its borders (Krasner, 1999, pp. 3-25).

Modern Greece, since gaining its independence from the Ottoman Empire in 1830, has been a weak country dependent upon great powers. The weakness of the country, its location, and the strategic interests of the Great Powers have invited foreign intervention in the affairs of Greece. An examination of the history and politics of modern Greece would reveal that most crises and important policy decisions were related to foreign pressure. Modern Greece has had a history of being involved in patron-client relationships, with Greece as the client and France, Russia, England, the United States and, since 1981, the European Community/European Union as the patrons.[2] As a client nation-state, Greece has had its sovereignty compromised by its patrons as well as by other more powerful nation-states.

This study focuses primarily on Westphalian and domestic sovereignty as related to modern Greece. Were Greek governments able to exclude foreign powers from meddling in Greece's affairs? How were these governments organized and how effective was the control exercised by those in power? In order to provide answers to these questions the work begins with Greek independence and follows the growth and maturation of the Greek nation-state to the present.

Chapter 1

War of Independence and Foreign Power Interference During the Nineteenth Century

While Napoleon was attempting to hold onto power, his enemies were meeting in the Congress of Vienna, at Vienna Austria (1814-1815) to decide on a settlement. Even though representatives from numerous European countries attended the Congress, it was the representatives of the Great Powers (Austria, England, Prussia, Russia, France) that dominated the meetings. The Congress of Vienna settled the boundaries of European states, attempted to maintain the traditional rulers to power, endeavored to preserve the status quo, strived to maintain the balance of power, and "established a new framework for international relations based on periodic meetings, or congresses, between the major powers" (Hunt, et al, 2001, p. 781). This congress system, also known as the Concert of Europe, was successful in accomplishing its goals and objectives at least between 1815-1848. In an effort to preserve the status quo, revolutions throughout Europe were not tolerated and were suppressed. One of the few successful revolutions during this period was the Greek revolution of 1821. The revolution would have failed if it were not for Russia's interest in the Ottoman Empire, the jealousies among the Great Powers, the determination of the Greeks to gain their independence, and the philhellenism among Europeans (Tatsios, 1984, p. 5) and to a lesser extent among Americans.

The Greek revolution began at a time when Europe was suffering from fatigue as a result of the Napoleonic Wars. As Crawley states (1973), "the outbreak of the Greek revolt in 1821 found Europe politically in a frame of mind half exhausted, half expectant, and in any case unsettled" (p. 1). In addition, the victorious powers did not want to hear anything about revolutions that would have threatened the balance of power and the status quo. Austria vigorously opposed the Greek revolution because the Sultan represented legitimacy and because the revolution would have given Russia the opportunity to interfere in the affairs of the Ottoman Empire, which was in the Russian plans. England agreed with Austria, also fearing Russian moves to the south (Vakalopoulos, 1987, pp. 167-168).

Prior to the revolution, the majority of the uneducated peasants in Greece were not interested in political independence. Their primary concern was safeguarding their rights and achieving protection from arbitrary landlords and officials. It is from this perspective that one must attempt to understand the role of the intelligentsia and more importantly the bourgeoisie in overthrowing the Ottoman oppressor (Mouzelis, 1978, p. 12). The Greek war for independence was organized first and foremost by the bourgeoisie "whose activities were as much based outside as within the Ottoman domains" (Clogg, 1992, p. 23). The bourgeoisie along with "intellectuals, teachers, and other professionals educated abroad, . . . acted as the catalyst which started the whole revolutionary process and gave it direction" (Mouzelis, 1978, pp. 12-13).

When the war for independence began, quarrels arose among the revolutionaries themselves. While the interests of the peasants were suppressed early in the war, there were important differences between the mainlanders and islanders on the one hand and the Peloponnesians on the other. The most strenuous disagreements were among factions of the upper classes: between the *traditionalists* and the *Westerners*. The *traditionalists,* with Eastern/Byzantine values, desired to overthrow the Ottomans without replacing or changing the government structure. The *Westerners* were nationalistic, and wanted a strong central government to reduce fragmentation and the autonomy of local chieftains (Kourvetaris & Dobratz, 1987, p. 36). At the conclusion of the revolution the *Westernizers* imposed their views upon the institutions of the new state. This was a result of their administrative and legal skills, and of the support that they, after the initial disapproval, received from European powers. The victory of the *Westernizers* explains the persisted attempts to create Western-liberal institutions. Of course, this does not mean that these institutions functioned the same way as in the West and it does not mean that the *traditionalists* altogether were kept out of power. Instead, they succeeded in infiltrating the state apparatus in order to safeguard and promote their interests (Mouzelis, 1978, pp. 13-14).

Merchants who had many contacts inside and outside Greece undertook the task of organizing and coordinating the different groups. An important step was taken when a group of three merchants (Nicholas Skouphas, Emmanuel Xanthos, Athanasios Tsakalov) in Russia established a secret organization called the *Philiki Etairia* or Friedly Society at Odessa in 1814 for the purpose of liberating Greece. The *Philiki Etairia* was not the first such organization. Rhigas Pheraios had founded an Etairia twenty years before, but it became void when he was captured by the Austrian authorities and was handed over to the Turks who executed him in 1798. Rhigas Pheraios and Adhamantios Koraes were among the first to stir Greek ideas of independence. Pheraios was born in Thessaly in 1757 and at the age of 23 he went to Wallachia. From there he left for Vienna in 1790 where he could express his revolutionary ideas. It is for two works that Pheraios is best known: a revolutionary hymn including an oath against tyranny, and a statement of the rights of man, combined with a proposed constitution for the new Greek republic (Brewer, 2001, p. 18).

The hymn begins:

> Shall we live in the mountain passes, like warriors of the old?
> Shall we live alone like lions, on the top of the mountain ridge?
> Shall we live in caves in darkness, shall slavery drive us away?
> Shall we say farewell to our family and to our beloved land?
> No! Better an hour of freedom, than forty years as a slave
> (Brewer, 2001, p. 18).

The oath begins:

> O Lord of all creation, I solemnly swear to Thee
> Never to act as tyrants do and never be slave to them

and concludes:

> And if this oath is broken, may lightning strike me down,
> And may I burnt to nothing, and vanish like smoke on the wind
> (Brewer, 2001, p. 18).

Pheraios' revolution was not just against the Turks, but all tyrants. He called upon Turks, Bulgarians, Albanians, Armenians, and others for assistance. His vision was based on the idea of the supremacy of the law, and he took the principles of the American and French revolutionary declarations and adapted them to Greek realities (Brewer, 2001, pp. 18-29).

Adhamantios Koraes was born in Smyrna in 1748. He hated the Turks; he had passion for learning, and believed that education had attributed to the success of the French Revolution. He also thought that the spread of education would allow the Greek movement for independence to succeed. He encouraged wealthy merchants to spend money-promoting education. His fanatical emphasis on education did not demonstrate any appreciation for the realities in Greece at the time, and his views about international matters were limited. "He blamed the powers of Europe, particularly Russia and England, for pursuing their own interests. It does not seem to have occurred to him that all nations, including the Greeks, pursued their own interests, and that salvation lay in finding ways to make the interests of other nations coincide with those of Greece. (Brewer, 2001, p. 25).

The *Philike Etairia* was a secret society and consisted of five levels. "In the lowest category, for the illiterate, were the Brothers. Next came the Associates (literally, the recommended ones), for the literate. Above them were the Priests, who could recruit to their own or to a lower grade. Next were the Shepherds, men of exceptional ability or wealth, and at the highest level of all was the Supreme Council, referred to as the Aorati Archi, the Invisible Directorate" (Brewer, 2001, p. 27).

The leaders of the *Philike Etairia* attempted to form a Greek national consciousness and to "foster among Greek patriots a spirit of resistance to the oppression of the Turkish government" (Cline, 1930, p. 10). In addition, the leaders of the *Philiki Etairia* were convinced that 1819-1820 was the right moment to start the revolution (Mavrogordato, 1931, p. 3; Woodhouse, 1991, pp. 130-131) for numerous reasons including the fact that in the 1820s there were revolutionary movements in Spain, Germany, France, Italy, Russia and even in Epirus where Ali Pasha was challenging the Sultan's authority.

The Greek revolution revealed that Greek nationalism had survived four hundred years of rule by the Ottoman Turks, who had occupied Greece since the fall of Constantinople in 1453. The Ottoman Empire was a Muslim state and was headed by the Sultan. The Christians were compelled to pay discriminatory taxes, were allowed to hold offices that did not have anything to do with Muslim affairs, and they were also considered to be inferior. Because the Ottoman Turks did not persecute the Christians, as long as they paid their taxes, the Greeks were able to retain their Greek Orthodox faith, their language and their customs. The Greeks also acquired power within the Ottoman Empire. For example, Greeks from the Phanar district of Constantinople called *phanariotes* occupied two influential offices: the chief interpreter of the council of ministers, who as the private secretary of the chief minister implemented the empire's foreign policy; and the private secretary to the Turkish minister of marine was in actuality the governor of the Greek islands. Together with the patriarch of Constantinople, these officers overlooked Greek religious, education, judicial and economic affairs of the Greeks, and had an input in the affairs of the Ottoman Empire (Pappas, 1985, pp. 1-2).

Most members of the *Philiki Etairia* believed that liberation would be achieved under the auspices of Russia. The leadership of the *Philiki Etairia* was first offered to Ioannis Kapodistrias, a Greek from Corfu who had served Tsar Alexander I as an alternate Minister of Foreign Affairs. When he refused to accept it because he considered the venture to be misguided and the timing wrong, in 1820 the leadership was offered to Alexander Ipsiladis who was also an aide to the Tsar and an officer in the Russian army. Ipsiladis accepted and immediately launched an uprising on March 6, 1821, with an army of 4,500 Serbs, Bulgarians, Montenegrins and 700 Greek students. He crossed the Pruth River from Russia into Moldavia and called upon all subjugated Christians in the Balkans to join his forces and fight for freedom and religion. Ipsiladis expected support from the Tsar, the Serbs, and others in the Danubian principalities. The Serbs, believing that Ipsiladis was only interested in establishing a Greek empire, refused to participate. Rumanian peasants participated only until they realized that Russia would not help. Ipsiladis appealed to Tsar Alexander I to become the liberator of the Greeks, but he disowned Ipsiladis and refused to help because the insurgency was disturbing the "Sultan's peace." The Tsar allowed Turkish forces to cross the Danube River and on June 19, 1821, the Turks defeated Ipsiladis' forces. He escaped to Vienna, Austria where he was imprisoned until 1827 and died the following year (Pappas, 1985, pp. 5-6). Ipsiladis' endeavor proved that there would not be a pan-Balkan uprising and that for the Greeks to succeed in gaining their independence they needed foreign assistance (Brewer, 2001, p. 61).

The defeat of Ipsiladis' forces did not signify the end of the revolutionary activities. In the same month as Ipsiladis' uprising, the Metropolitan of Patras, Germanos, proclaimed according to Greek legend the rising in the Peloponnese on March 25, 1821, the feast day of the Annunciation, which is now celebrated as Greece's national day (Woodhouse, 1991, p. 134). For the first three years of the revolution, the Greeks were able to hold their own against the Ottoman Turks. Trouble came when disputes arose among the revolutionaries. Although no dominant personality emerged to take command, the revolution persisted as a "fragmented effort." The only unifying element seemed to be the common hatred of the Ottoman Turks and the determination to gain independence (Kousoulas, 1974, pp. 10-11). Incited by the cry, "In the Morea shall no Turk be left, nor in the whole wide world," the Greeks fought the Turks with intensity, cruelty and courage. Ruthless massacres of Turks took place wherever the Greeks gained control. At Tripolitza, the capital of the Morea, approximately twelve thousand Turks were killed. It was these actions that led Adamantios Koraes "to urge his countrymen that, although they were fighting Turks, they should not follow Turkish practices in dealing with the enemy" (Cline, 1930, p. 11).

Meanwhile, the Ottoman Turks did not remain silent. The Sultan ordered the murder of Greeks serving as officials in Constantinople, and hanged the patriarch of the Greek Church, Gregorios, on Easter Sunday, 1821, shocking Christians. "It is estimated, that during the first three months of the revolution, 30,000 Greeks fell victims to the furry and fanaticism of their tyrants" (Tennent, 1845, p. li). The victims were chosen not because of their support of the revolution, but simply because of the fact that they were Christian Greeks. In Cyprus, almost the entire Greek Orthodox Church hierarchy was executed (Borowiec, 1983, p. 22). Terrible destruction was caused everywhere and a clear example was the devastation of and the massacre at the Aegean island of Chios. The incident at Chios received much publicity and ignited outrage in Western Europe and the United States against the Ottoman Turks, and as a result brought aid to the Greeks.

Initially, the Greeks' strive for independence left all European governments unmoved and the official European view was that the Greeks were rebellious subjects of the Sultan. But the execution of the patriarch and the massacre of Christian Greeks in Chios and elsewhere finally attracted the attention of the Tsar who viewed himself as the protector of the Orthodox Church. "Accordingly Russia's first intervention was specifically concerned with the inviolability of the Christian religion, and the demands presented by the Russian Ambassador at Constantinople in July 1821 only incidentally mentioned the Greek insurgents, in order to contemplate their submission within a given time. Russia was looking for an opportunity to confirm and extend her own rights of encroachment, spiritually in the Orthodox Church and geographically in the principalities of Wallachia and Moldavia, while the other Powers, led by Castlereagh and Metternich, were worthily active in what is called 'avoiding a European conflagration'" (Mavrogordato, 1931, pp. 15-16).

The Greek revolution placed all European powers in a difficult position. The weakness of the Ottoman Empire, and the Sultan's inability to assure political and administrative stability in his territories in and around the eastern Mediterranean troubled the Europeans. "But neither could any power come to the rescue of the Greeks without finding itself in war with others. Their national interests regarding the Ottoman Empire and the Greeks were politically and commercially in conflict. England, France and Austria had extensive trade with the empire, whereas Russia desired to weaken and destroy the empire, England wanted to continue to enjoy its most favored commercial status in it, France to regain her seventeenth century commercial preeminence in it, and Austria to further her extensive commerce. They could not help the Greeks without damaging their commercial interests and influence with the Turks—and they could not weaken Turkey without exposing her to Russian aggression" (Pappas, 1985, pp. 16-17).

In the summer of 1821, Russia and the Ottoman Empire were close to war. As long as Tsar Alexander I was under the influence of Metternich, the Tsar opposed the Greek revolution for being supported, like other revolutions in Europe, by liberals based in Paris. But upon return to Russia, he changed his mind. A group of advisors, including John Kapodistrias, the Tsar's Foreign Minister, convinced Alexander I to support the Greeks and take action against the Turks. The Great Powers of Europe—Austria, England, Prussia, and France—recognizing that it was to their interest to preserve the Ottoman Empire, attempted to restrain the Tsar. Determined not to abandon the Greeks, Tsar Alexander decided to act alone. In the fall of 1825, he began preparations for war with the Ottomans. When he died on December 1, 1825, his successor and brother Nicholas I continued preparations for war. But he also returned to a policy of acting in concert with England and France (Pappas, 1985, pp. 17-19).

Of all the Great European Powers, Russia enjoyed the strongest relationship with the Greeks. The most powerful connection was, of course, the common Orthodox faith. In addition, as Russia and the Ottoman Empire, with common lengthy boundaries, were drawn into a closer relationship during the eighteenth century, the Russians found it necessary to resort to the Greeks who worked for the Sultan in many official capacities to behave as translators and intermediaries. Furthermore, economic interests fostered a symbiotic relationship between the Russians and the Greeks. Greek merchants, during the nineteenth century, dominated commerce throughout the empire. Greek ships carried Russian grain and had the right to fly the Russian flag. Greeks established merchant colonies around Europe and the Russian government appointed Greeks as consuls throughout the Balkans (Jelavich, 1987, pp. 75-76).

Even though friction was abundant among the revolutionaries, the Greeks were able to hold their own against the Ottomans from 1821 to 1825. Unfortunately, however, the Greeks also had great difficulties establishing and maintaining an effective civil government. "In 1822, a 'national' assembly proclaimed the independence of Greece and announced a constitution. This marked the first of series of attempts to create a central government. The constitution—a document reported in America as modeled after that of the United States—provided for a republican form of government, equality before the law, religious toleration and freedom of the press. However admirable such a plan may have been in theory, it was in fact utterly unfitted to existing conditions in Greece. Actually chaos prevailed. Jealousy among the leaders was rampant. There was lacking any effective central authority. Civil conflict ensued between the partisan chiefs and the aristocratic elements of the population" (Cline, 1930, pp. 12-13).

While the Greeks were fighting among themselves, the Sultan called upon his vassal, the pasha of Egypt, for help. The arrival of the Egyptian forces changed the course of the revolution in favor of the Ottomans. In 1826, the pasha's forces overcame Mesologhi in northwestern Greece. When the Sultan's forces captured Athens a year later, the Greek cause was in danger. It was at that critical point when Greek leaders realized the gravity of the situation and were convinced that foreign power intervention was necessary to gain their independence. At approximately the same time, Russia as well as England and France changed their stance toward the Greek revolution and decided to support the Greek cause at the expense of the Sultan. The governments of the three Great Powers concluded that an independent Greece would not harm their interests and would not threaten their security. Besides, these states wished to protect their commercial and strategic interests in the eastern Mediterranean, and each was suspicious of the others. For the purpose of preventing unilateral actions by one Great Power, which might hurt the others, the three decided to act together as mediators (Fry & Raymond, 1983, p. 56).

In April 1826, the governments of Russia and England offered their mediation services providing that the Sultan recognized Greece as a tributary dependency. England's foreign secretary, George Canning, described this policy as one of "peaceful interference" (Clogg, 1992, p. 42). The Sultan rejected the proposal and the conditions in Greece became even worse. On July 6, 1827, England, France and Russia signed the Treaty of London demanding the recognition of Greek independence by the Turks and sent a joint fleet to support the Greek revolution. The Sultan responded by calling for additional forces from Egypt and the Allied Powers destroyed the Turkish fleet at the battle of Navarino in October 1827. In 1828, Russia sent troops into Ottoman land, what is known as Romania today, and then in September 1829 gained control of that territory with the Treaty of Adrianople. As a result of the treaty, France, England and Russia, the "Protecting Powers," were able to decide the future of Greece. The Turks were compelled to recognize the independence of a small Greece and in 1830 a second Treaty of London declared Greece as an independent kingdom. As Merriman (1996) eloquently states: "After the battle of Navarino in 1827, the allies had actually apologized to the Turkish sultan for sinking his fleet. In doing so, they acknowledged a paradox: the allies of the Concert of Europe had intervened militarily on behalf of a nationalist movement against an established power. The Greek revolt had shattered the Congress system. Like Delacroix's painting, the allied intervention had sanctioned a noble act" (p. 1361).

The Greek revolution became one of the most famous in Europe and it evoked popular sympathy among philhellenes in the United States and especially Western Europe. Popular support in the United States threatened American neutrality and isolation. As the Secretary of State, John Quincy Adams, maintained the policy of neutrality and isolation. But as President, he changed his stance toward the Greek revolution to one of "benevolent neutrality" by sending agents to Greece and by providing financial assistance to the new government (Pappas, 1985, p. vii).

Philhellenic societies were founded in almost all European countries and the United States. "Liberals through out Europe, who were seeing their own hopes crushed at home, imagined that the ancient Greek culture, and democracy were being born" (Kagan, et al., 1995, p. 782). Educated Europeans and Americans admired ancient Greek culture, and Russians were moved by the piety of their Orthodox brethren. Many Europeans and Americans supported the Greek cause because it was a struggle for liberty and self-determination. They also supported the Greek revolution because of the American and French revolutions and the emphasis on freedom, fraternity, and independence. Furthermore, they championed the Greek revolution because of romanticism-an emotional attitude toward life and a devotion to the common people. The influence of romanticism was manifested in the actions of many individuals including Lord Byron who went to Greece and fought on the side of the revolutionaries and died in Greece in 1824 (Cline, 1930, pp. 15-17).

Despite the small population and territorial size of Greece, the Greek revolution had an important impact on European affairs. "It disrupted the Concert of Europe and the Holy Alliance. In a diplomatic revolution, Russia and France abandoned Austria and Prussia to align with England for the Greek cause. It brought the first significant change on the map of Europe following the Congress of Vienna, and it was the first great victory for the principle of nationality after 1815. It was hailed by the liberals of all nations as a victory over conservatism and legitimacy. It gave rise to what was thereafter referred to as the Eastern Question. The gradual disintegration of the Ottoman Empire, through a series of national revolutions in the nineteenth and early twentieth centuries, set off vigorous competition among the major powers-Russia, Austria, England, and France-for control of the Balkan nationalities and the Turks, and gave rise to a series of crises and wars which eventually led to the First World War" (Pappas, 1985, p. 26).

Kapodistrias and his Assassination

The rivalries among the insurgents during the initial stages of the revolution did not prevent them from making an effort to write a constitution and establish a central government. Their attempts were partly successful. A constitution was enacted in January, 1822 in Epidaurus, but the government was too weak. The Greeks endeavored to write another constitution that would set up a strong central government. By the time the constitutional assembly met at Troezena, the revolution was at its lowest point. The Secretary of the Troezena Assembly, Spiliades, said that a government did not exist except in name only, and that a civil war threatened the country. The chaotic conditions did not deter the Assembly from producing in 1827 an important document that tried to maintain a balance between democratic principles and effective government. The delegates attending the meetings were influenced by the ideals of the French Revolution and the American Constitution. The Troezena Constitution provided a *Kyvernitis* or President, who was to be elected every seven years by male voters and who was to be, as the president of the United States, both the head of government and the head of state. The single-chamber legislature called *Vouli,* whose members were to be elected every three years, was entrusted with the enactment of laws (Kousoulas, 1974, pp. 11-14). In 1827, Ioannis Kapodistrias, a former minister of the Tsar, was elected as the first *Kyvernitis*, an office he assumed in 1828.

Kapodistrias used his diplomatic skills to secure as much territory as possible for the new state and to lay the foundations of a state structure. "For him, modernity required a bureaucratic and centralized state administering an enlightened law code. In his administration, Western education would be liberating and necessary, but traditional religious values and practices would also remain" (Legg & Roberts, 1997, p. 28). Those who had held local power during the years of Ottoman rule and those whose reputation and prestige had been enhanced during the years of the revolution wanted to preserve their positions and were not ready to accept a strong central government and the authoritarian style of Kapodistrias. Kapodistrias, who had contempt for the Greek elites and believed that the Greeks were not capable of self-government, believed that the constitution was too liberal for a country that was under Ottoman rule for four hundred years and had just finished fighting a savage war for independence. He decided that the circumstances called for drastic action. Within a few days he pressured the *Vouli* to suspend the new constitution and to vote itself out of existence for the foreseeable future. Most people in Greece, hoping for peace and stability, went along with Kapodistrias and considered him as a savior (Kousoulas, 1974, pp. 15-16).

Kapodistrias succeeded in imposing a personal dictatorship. His foreign policy was closely allied to Russian interests. Even though domestically he proved unable to solve the numerous problems facing Greece, his government was the first serious attempt to organize the new state. He was among the first to care about public education, he tried to curb piracy, to organize the administration and to impose some control regarding the mutinous spirit of the notables. For that reason he confronted a lot of opposition from those affected by his policies including the notables, many of the islanders and liberal intellectuals. Encouraged by representatives of France and England who distrusted Kapodistrias for being too close to Russia, the opponents of the first *Kyvernitis* assassinated him on his way to church at Nafplion, the provisional capital, on October 9, 1831 (Svoronos, 1976, pp. 72-73).

Monarchy

Conditions in Greece were worsened after the assassination of Kapodistrias and "within Greece the stage was set for the adoption of the foreign sponsored idea of a monarchy" (Carey & Carey, 1968, p. 84). "The Greeks' innate sense of equality, and the rivalry among the leading families, made the idea of one of themselves becoming head of state quite inconceivable. No self-respecting Greek would accept another fellow countryman as his or her sovereign" (der Kriste, 1994, p. 1). The state of anarchy convinced at least some Greeks that a monarchy might be the answer. France, England and Russia, the Protecting Powers, however, founded the monarchy. "When the republic ended in calamity, the powers indicated that they had contributed decisively to Greek independence . . . and they had not only the right but the obligation to intervene" (Carey & Carey, 1968, p. 84). The Great Powers decided that Greece should be an hereditary monarchy, whose king should be drawn from one of the royal houses of Europe not directly connected with those of England, Russia, or France. After Leopold of Saxe-Coburg, discouraged by Kapodistrias' bleak reports, by the small territorial size of Greece and fearing that he would be unpopular in Greece, had turned down the throne, the Great Powers' choice was Otto of Wittelsbach, the seventeen-year-old son of King Ludwig of Bavaria. "It was symptomatic of the dependent nature of the new state that the Greeks were not a party to the treaty of May 1832 between Britain, France, Russia and Bavaria under which King Otto was to accept the throne and which placed Greece under the 'guarantee' of the Protecting Powers" (Clogg, 1992, p. 47).

This was the beginning of direct and indirect intervention in the affairs of the Greek state by foreign powers. "Ultimately, the Great Powers, exercising a paternalism that was to recur throughout much of Modern Greek history, determined the boundaries and governmental form of the new state" (Legg & Roberts, 1997, p. 29). Otto was offered the crown by the Great Powers, not Greece. In addition, it was during this period when the so-called "English," "French," and "Russian" political parties were born. The leaders of these parties looked toward the three major European powers for support to accomplish Greek national goals. These parties did not have stable leadership and their supporters did not hesitate to switch parties for personal gains (Vakalopoulos, 1987, p. 212).

After coronation as Othon (the Greek form of his name), King of Greece, he became a strong supporter of Greek aspirations, hopes, and desires. In spite of the Byzantine and Ottoman background of administration, King Othon "tried to apply patterns of administration which had been developed in well-ordered communities of central Europe to the small, war-ravaged Balkan state. . . . This situation, which had no parallel in any other Balkan country, proved disastrous for the early years of Greek political life" (Jelavich & Jelavich, 1965, p. 62). Officials were nominated by, responsible to and removed by the king. If left alone, the Greeks would have been capable of developing their own institutions. But because they were not familiar with western methods of governing and because they were not comfortable with western dress-code, they were "completely ignored and became merely the subjects of a western system above their heads, which was in effect a Bavarian protectorate. Not only the Greeks themselves but their municipal institutions were ignored by the new administration, which imposed prefects, sub-prefects and demarchs (mayors) all nominated by the Ministry of the Interior. It has been said that Greece never recovered from this western reform initiated by Kapodistrias, for its government suffered ever since, and continues to suffer . . . , from excessive centralization" (Mavrogordato, 1931, pp. 34-35). Beginning with Othon's years Greece became locked in a centralized system, which has always been a reason for a "slow-moving and creaking governmental machinery" (Carey & Carey, 1968, p. 85).

Othon ruled the individualistic Greeks as an absolute ruler. Although he believed that he was forwarding the causes of the Greeks, he became increasingly unpopular. He insisted upon seeing everything and became so involved in details to cause the delay of signing even urgent documents. He did not trust anyone, not even himself (Vakalopoulos, 1987, p. 242). A group of politicians, insurrectionary leaders, and some members of the military launched a coup against Othon in September 1843. (See Table 1 about the fate of Greek monarchs) As a result of the coup, the King agreed to a new constitution. The document, drawn up in 1844, set up a two-chambered (the *Vouli* and the *Gerousia*) legislative assembly and established a constitutional monarchy. Both chambers could not pass laws without approval, and executive power was in the hands of a Council of Ministers appointed and dismissed by the monarch at his discretion. Also, the 1844 constitution shown respect for the rights of citizens but did not include any sanctions against those who did violate them (Kousoulas, 1990, p. 7). The 1844 constitution, although distorted in practice, was the first to allow the development of a primitive parliamentary system (Alivizatos, 1990, p. 132). The conversion to a constitutional monarchy did not necessarily lessen the King's powers. He controlled the upper house by nominating all its members for life; he had the power to veto any legislation he did not approve; he governed by executive decree; and he had the power of appointment and dismissal of ministers. The King succeeded in building a personal political machine (Carey & Carey, 1968, p. 86).

TABLE 1
The Fate of Greek Monarchs

Othon I	• Prince Otto, second son of King Ludwig of Bavaria, becomes King of Greece with a Regency Council in 1832
	• Forced to accept constitution in 1844
	• Forced out in 1864 and a provisional government declared his reign at an end
George I	• Prince William, second son of King Christian IX of Denmark, ascends throne as King of the Hellenes in 1864 and Greece is classified as Crowned Democracy
	• Assassinated by madman in Thessaloniki in 1913
Constantine I	• Succeeds father as King of the Hellenes in 1913
	• Forced into exile in 1917, accompanied by Crown Prince George
Alexander I	• Second son declared King of the Hellenes in 1917
	• Dies after bite from pet monkey in 1920
Constantine I	• Returns after plebiscite in 1920
	• Abdicates in favor of Crown Prince George in 1922
George II	• Succeeds father as King of the Hellenes in 1922
	• Republic proclaimed in 1924; King George II exiled
	• Plebiscite restores monarchy in 1935; King George II returns Italian and German occupation begins in 1941; George II heads government-in-exile
	• Plebiscite of 1946; George II returns
	• George II dies in 1947 and is succeeded by brother
Paul I	• King of the Hellenes in 1947
	• Paul dies in 1964 and is succeeded by son
Constantine II	• King of the Hellenes in 1964
	• Goes into exile after abortive "counter-coup" against military dictatorship; regency declared
	• Military dictatorship declares King "deposed" in 1973
	• Plebiscite on the monarchy in 1974; republic declared
	• King and royal family remain in exile

Source: Data from Keith R. Legg & John M. Roberts (1977). *Modern Greece: A Civilization on the Periphery*, p. 59. Boulder, Colorado: Westview Press.

King Othon's relations with the Protecting Powers were difficult. England did not approve his strong pro-Hellenic stand and his refusal to assist in strengthening the Ottoman Empire, which England needed as an ally against Russia. Russia, strongly Orthodox in religion, was critical of Othon because he remained a Roman Catholic. Both England and Russia opposed his passionate support of the *Megali Idea* or Great Idea[3], with its desire to expand Greece's boundaries. Napoleon III of France believed that King Othon incited constant insurrections throughout the Balkans hoping to expand Greek territory (Carey & Carey, 1968, p. 87). By the early 1850s, a new generation of Greeks was reaching maturity who had no involvement in the war for independence and who did not have much in common with politicians who ruthlessly pursued power and wanted to control the state, the largest employer in the country, in order to provide jobs and do favors to their clients. At the same time, the "English," the "French," and the "Russian" parties began to fade away.

The supporters of the *Megali Idea* believed that the Great Power politics of the period provided an opportunity to realize the "national dreams." Napoleon III of France was determined to promote French interests in the Middle East to the annoyance of the Russians. The French demand that the Ottomans grant privileges to Catholics in the Holy Land at the expense of Orthodox Christians infuriated Tsar Nicholas I who considered himself the protector of all Orthodox Christians in the Ottoman Empire under the terms of the 1774 Treaty of Kuchuk-Kainardji. When the Sultan decided to accept the French demands, the Tsar declared war against the Ottomans and in August 1853 Russian troops invaded Moldavia and Wallachia. This was the beginning of what is known as the Crimean War (Kousoulas, 1974, p. 30). Othon's relationship with the Great Powers deteriorated even further by his decision to support Russia. In 1854, England and France, and later Austria and Piedmont-Sardinia, declared war against Russia to protect their own national interests and to maintain the balance-of-power in Europe. French and English troops landed in Crimea in 1854 and the city fell a year later. The Russian army was defeated and as a result of the Peace of Paris, signed on March 30, 1856, Russia lost the right to have naval bases in the Straits of Dardanelles and the Black Sea. Moldavia and Walachia, which merged to become Romania, became autonomous Turkish provinces under the protection of the victors.

The involvement of the Ottoman Empire in the Crimean War galvanized the Greeks and revived the *Megali Idea*. Many Greek volunteers crossed the border with the Ottoman Empire into Thessaly, Epirus, and Macedonia. The European powers wished to defend the territorial integrity of the Empire, and England and France blockaded Greece and landed troops at Pireaus, the port of Athens, between 1854 and 1857 to pressure the Greek government to stop stirring problems within the Ottoman Empire and to remain neutral in the war. King Othon had no choice but to agree, and Mavrokordatos, the new Prime Minister of Greece, declared Greece's neutrality and recalled all troops operating in northern Greece (Gregoriades, 1979, pp. 43-47). Coming just four years after the Don Pacifico[4] incident, this was one of the worst examples of foreign power interference in the domestic affairs of Greece. On many occasions during the years of occupation the Protecting Powers degraded the Greek monarchy and that, of course, made Othon more popular among his subjects (Tatsios, 1984, p. 25).

In 1858 King Othon celebrated the twenty-fifth anniversary of his accession to the throne, but four years later he was forced to leave the country. Othon's popularity quickly evaporated for a variety of reasons. First, he constantly interfered with the formation of governments and he was highly secretive. Second, he was unable to accomplish the "national dreams" associated with the *Megali Idea*-unlike Cavour who had succeeded in unifying Italy. Third, during the revolutionary war in Italy in 1859 Othon supported the wrong side. Even though the people of Greece were supportive of the insurgents in Italy, the King was more sympathetic to the interests of the Austrians. Fourth, there was a question of succession. Othon did not have an heir and because no Bavarian prince had entered the Orthodox Church, legally there was no heir since the 1844 constitution required that the successor must be of the Christian Orthodox faith. Fifth, the people of Greece had begun to realize that the representative form of government did not provide them with greater liberty and no power to express their opinion as long as the government was controlled and manipulated by those above-what they referred to as "the System" (Mavrogordato, 1931, pp. 50-52). Multiple rebellions through out the country followed with the most significant occurring at Nafplion on February 1862, which was ultimately suppressed. But a new rebellion began at Mesologhi and Patras spread to Athens. When King Othon and Queen Amalia attempted to return to Pireaus from a tour around the Peloponnese, they could not land at Pireaus where his own soldiers had killed the royalist commandant. In addition, a revolutionary triumvirate of Kanaris, Voulgaris, and Rouphos was in power in

Athens. Othon, in order to avoid more bloodshed, abdicated and returned to Bavaria (Mavrogordato, 1931, p. 53; Vakalopoulos, 1987, pp. 256-257) where he died in obscurity in 1867 at the age of fifty-two, "still wearing the *foustanella*, the national dress of Greece, and professing his affection for the country" (Papacosma, 1977, p. 7).

Chapter 2

Vasilevomene Demokratia

Neither domestic nor international forces seriously opposed the 1862 developments. The Greek National Assembly approved the nomination of Prince Alfred, son of Queen Victoria of England, but the Greeks did not yet have the right to choose their own monarch. England vetoed the decision because of the agreement with the other Protecting Powers that no candidate should be chosen who was a member of the reigning family of one of the Protecting Powers. England was also fearful that its relationship with the Ottoman Empire would be negatively affected by becoming so close to Greece. The Greeks, realizing that it would be difficult for them to find a candidate acceptable to England as well as to France and Russia, asked England for assistance. On March 30 it was announced that England had found a king for the Greeks in the person of Prince William George, son of the heir to the Danish throne of the house of Glucksborg. The Greek branch of the same dynasty reigned intermittently between 1863 and 1874. The decision was formalized on July 13, 1863, with a treaty between England, France, Russia, and Denmark, which declared that Greece under the guarantee of the Protecting Powers "forms a monarchical, independent and constitutional state." In this treaty there was an emphasis on the constitutional nature of the Greek government, which meant to imply that the king would not be a figurehead, would not pursue expansionist policies and would ferment revolutionary activities in Europe. The treaty further stated that the successors of the king would always be Greek Orthodox and that the kingdoms of Greece and Denmark would never be united (Mavrogordato, 1931, pp. 56-57).

Prince William George was elected King in 1863 by the National Assembly and was crowed as King George I (1863-1913) of the Hellenes and not of Greece as in the case of Othon before a new constitution was drawn up. The designation King of the Hellenes was important because now the new King "appeared to embody the political existence and national aspirations of all Greeks, not simply those living within the frontiers of the small kingdom" (Tatsios, 1984, p. 28). King George landed in Greece on October 30, 1863, and took the oath to the new constitution on November 20, 1864. In spite of early inclinations to reign as an absolute ruler, King George I learned how to rule in accordance with the 1864 constitution. The 1864 document introduced universal male suffrage, a unicameral legislature (the Crown appointed *Gerousia* was abolished) responsible for enacting laws, and the notion of popular sovereignty was enhanced even more by the provision that the king had no other powers than those granted to him by the constitution and the laws. The constitution also preserved the right of the monarch to appoint and dismiss the cabinet (Kousoulas, 1973, p. 9). King George had a limited formal role in domestic policy but retained important powers in regards to foreign policy. It is important to point out that the constitution of 1864, with which crowned democracy or *vasilevomene demokratia* was introduced replacing constitutional monarchy or *syntagmatike monarchia*, remained approximately the same until the coup d' etat of April 21, 1967, and it was, at least on paper, one of the most egalitarian in Europe during the nineteenth century (Alivizatos, 1990, p. 132).

Numerous political parties competed for power and political leaders, once in office, found it difficult to put their proposals into practice. Two politicians dominated the political scene at the end of the nineteenth century: Charilaos Trikoupes and Theodore Deligiannes. While the former wished to follow a moderate foreign policy and to concentrate on the economic development of Greece, the latter emphasized foreign policy issues. The creation of the Bulgarian state was viewed as a threat to the interests of Greece because of conflicting claims related to Macedonia. The Greeks were also disappointed with the outcome at the Congress of Berlin. Even though they gained Thessaly and part of Epirus in 1881, they had hoped for more. Furthermore, England, in order to promote its interests in the eastern Mediterranean, colonized the island of Cyprus, which was inhabited mainly by Greeks (Jelavich & Jelavich, 1965, pp. 63-64).

Deligianes (See Table 2 about Prime Ministers after the 1843 constitution) returned to power on April 28, 1895, and for the next two years he had to deal with the demands of foreign creditors. National pride was very much wounded and many in Greece accused the foreign financiers for treating Greece as a common debtor knowing the contributions Greece had made to Western Civilization. The Greeks also believed that the many humiliations that Greece had to go through were a result of the small territorial size of the country, a territorial size that was imposed by foreign powers. The only way out of this situation was to pursue irredentist policies to expand the territory of Greece. For the purpose of mobilizing public support a secret society was formed called the *Ethnike Etairia* or National Society. Within a brief period of time the organization succeeded in getting the support of many important personalities and it gave a new impetus to the *Megali Idea*. With Trikoupes' moderation gone, the field was open to those who wanted to liberate Greeks subject to foreign occupation. In 1896 the Ottomans received much criticism for atrocities committed against the Armenians and many in Greece thought that the time was right to take a bold action (Kousoulas, 1974, p. 81).

TABLE 2
Greek Prime Ministers Since the 1843 Constitution

Andreas Metaxas 1843-1844
Alex. Mavrokordatos 1844
Ioannis Kolettis 1844-1847
Kitsos Tzavellas 1847-1848
G. Kountouriotis 1848
Konstant. Kanaris 1848-1849, 1865
Anto. Kriezis 1849-1854
Dim. Voulgaris 1855-1857, 1862-1867, 1871, 1874
Athan. Miaoulis 1857-1862
Ioannis Kolokotronis 1862
Zinovios Valvis 1863, 1864
Diomidis Kyriakos 1863
Venizelos Roufos 1863, 1865
Alex. Koumoundouros 1865-1866, 1870, 1875, 1876, 1877, 1878, 1880
Epamein. Deligeorgis 1865-1870, 1872, 1876, 1877
Aristeidis Moraitinis 1867-1868
Thrasyvoulos Zaimis 1869-1870, 1871
Charilaos Trikoupes 1875-1878, 1880, 1882, 1892, 1893
Theodore Deligianes 1885-1890, 1895

Dim. Valvis 1886
Kon. Konstantopoulos 1892
Sot. Sotiropoulos 1893
Nikol. Deligiannes 1895
Dimitrios Rallis 1897-1905, 1906
Alex. Zaimis 1897-1899, 1915
Georg. Theotokis 1899-1903, 1905, 1908
Kyriak. Mavromihalis 1909-1910
Stef. Dragoumis 1910
Elef. Venizelos 1910-1915, 1917-1920, 1928-1932
Dim. Gounaris 1915, 1922
Stef. Skouloudis 1915-1916
Nikol. Kalogeropoulos 1916
Spyr. Lampros 1916-1917
E. Repoulis 1917
Ioan. Tsirimokos 1917
Nikol. Stratos 1922
Pet. Protopapadakis 1922
Nikol. Traintafyllakos 1922
Anast. Charalampis 1922
Sotir. Krokidas 1922
Styl. Gonatas 1922-1924
G. Kafantaris 1924
Alex. Papanastasiou 1924
Themist. Sophoulis 1924, 1945, 1946, 1947, 1949
Andr. Michalakopoulos 1924-1925
Theod. Pangalos 1925
A.Eftaxias 1926
Georg. Kondylis 1926
Panagis Tsaldaris 1932-1933, 1933-1935
Alex. Othonaios 1933
Const. Demertzis 1935-1936
Ioan. Metaxas 1936 (From 8/4/1936 to 1/29/1941 Dictator)
Alex. Korizis 1941
G. Tsolakoglou 1941-1942 (German Occupation)
K. Logothetopoulos 1942-1943 (German Occupation)
I.Rallis 1943-1945 (German Occupation)
Emman. Tsouderos 1941-1944
Sophoklis Venizelos 1944, 1950, 1951

Georg. Papandreou 1944-1945, 1963, 1964
Nikol. Plastiras 1945, 1950
Petros Voulgaris 1945
Arciepiskopos Damaskinos 1945
Panag. Kanellopoulos 1945, 1967
Panag. Poulitsas 1946
Dimitrios Maximos 1947
Konst. Tsaldaris 1947
Alex. Diomidis 1949
A.Kyriakos 1949-1950
Ioannis Theotokis 1950
Dim. Kiousopoulos 1952
Alex. Papagos 1952-1955
Konst. Karamanlis 1955-1961, 1974-1980
K. Georgakopoulos 1958
Konst. Dovas 1961
Panag. Pipinelis 1963
Styl. Mavromihalis 1963
Io. Paraskevopoulos 1963-1964, 1966
Georg. Novas 1965
Ilias Tsirimokos 1965
Stef. Stefanopoulos 1965-1966
K. Kollias 1967
G. Papadopoulos 1967-1973 (Dictator)
S. Markezinis 1973
A.Androutsopoulos 1973-1974
Georg. Rallis 1980-1981
Andreas Papandreou 1981-1987, 1993-1996

Source: Data from Epameinondas K. Stasinopoulos (1985). *Kommata Kai Ekloges Sten Hellada: 1821-1985,* p. 7. Athens: Epameinondas K. Stasinopoulos; Enoses Teos Voulefton (1985). *150 Chronia Hellenikes Democratias*, pp. 219-220. Athens: Hellenoekdotike.

Tzannetakis 1989
I.Grivas 1989
Xenophon Zolotas 1989-1990
Constantine Mitsotakis 1990-1993
Costas Simitis 1996-Present

Defeat of 1897

There had been many revolts during the nineteenth century on the island of Crete, which was part of the Ottoman Empire. Each one was about union or *enosis* with Greece and each one was destined to fail because of English opposition to changing the status of the island. For six years after the 1889 revolt the Christians on the island lived under many restrictions. Fearing another rebellion, the Sultan decided to relax these restrictions and at this time it was the Muslims who were angered by the Sultan's actions. They attacked Christians and in response the Christians formed a revolutionary committee. Even though Prime Minister Deligiannes uncharacteristically asked the people of Crete for moderation, violence erupted. In Greece there was such popular outrage that even the King, a moderate man, decided to mobilize forces. Foreign allies made suggestions to accept autonomy for Crete, but the Greeks and the Cretans immediately rejected the suggestions. In 1897, news of more massacres in Crete further excited the public. The pressure from the public and parliament was so great that Deligiannes announced on February 10, 1897, that troops under the command of Prince George, the King's second son were on their way to Crete. Five days later additional troops were sent to the island and the people of Greece received the news with great enthusiasm (Kousoulas, 1974, p. 82). The decision in 1897 to go to war against the Ottomans proved to be disastrous and in the spring of the same year the Ottoman forces soundly defeated the unprepared Greek army. Greece was financially bankrupt, militarily unprepared, and fought against a Turkish army which had been recently reorganized by German officers (Couloumbis, et al., p. 31). The Ottoman forces invaded Greek territory, and only intervention by the Great Powers rescued the country and the monarchy. Important strategic territories were returned to the Ottoman Empire along the northern frontier. Military defeat and the financial problems that followed forced the Greek government to accept even more control by outside powers. The foreign powers "instituted a Commission of Control over sufficient revenues to serve the interest of the indemnity to Turkey and of older national debts also. One half of the Cretan problem was settled (November 1898) by a four-Power occupation of the chief towns and by appointing as High Commissioner the Greek King's second son, Prince George, who did much to pacify the island and to make its autonomy a reality. After a disagreement with his Cretan councilor, Eleftherios Venizelos, and a proclamation of union with Greece by the Cretan opposition, Prince George resigned in 1906: the island was rapidly and peacefully hellenized under his successor, and the remaining international troops were withdrawn. . . ." (Heurtley, et al, 1965, pp. 106-107).

The aftermath of the 1897 defeat was a period of frustration for the Greeks. During 1897-1909 Greece was very much isolated. In 1897, the Greek government attempted to secure German military advisors, but the Ottoman Sultan, who was aligned with Kaiser Wilhelm II, vetoed the idea. In 1903, Russia attempted to garner European support for a Cretan settlement favorable to Greece. The Greeks held back because they feared that Russia would use its actions regarding Crete as a justification for concessions for the Slavs in Macedonia. King George I unsuccessfully sought alliances with Austria, Italy, France, and England. There were many reasons for the failure to end the isolation: First, Greece was of little military value to the European powers. Second, each European power's relationship with other powers in Europe and elsewhere seemed to be more important than a possible relationship with Greece. Third, the Greeks were unwilling to accept strings attached to such possible relationships (Couloumbis, et al., 1976, pp. 32-33).

The 1897 defeat also symbolized the weaknesses of the political leadership, and the lack of direction and strength to effectively manage the problems confronting Greece. But "the greater their division, uncertainty, and sense of grievance about the imperfections of their own society, the more unquestioned was their unity of purpose, at least in an expressive sense, in relation to the Great Idea; and more specifically to the fate of Macedonia, Epirus, and Crete" (Campbell & Sherrard, 1968, p. 109). These aspirations were much affected by the revolutionary movement of young Turkish officers; their official name was the Committee of Union and Progress, who overthrew Sultan Abdul Hamid in early July 1908. Even though the Young Turks claimed to be liberal and to recognize the rights of other nationalities within the Empire, they expected loyalty to the state. The Balkan nations and some of their neighbors took advantage of the situation in the Ottoman Empire. On October 5, 1908, Bulgaria declared its independence from the Ottoman Empire and Bosnia-Herzegovina was annexed the following day by Austria. Two days later the Cretans announced the union of Crete with Greece. The Greek government, having in mind the presence of the foreign powers in Greece and remembering the disaster of 1897, was reluctant to support the actions of the Cretans. The Young Turks, unable to do much regarding Bulgaria and Bosnia-Herzegovina, were determined to suppress developments in Crete. The Cretans raised the Greek flag and when the Ottomans threatened, the Prime Minister of Greece, Rallis, said that he could not control the developments and the foreign powers sent 250 marines to Crete and lowered the Greek flag (Campbell & Sherrard, 1968, pp. 109-110).

Revolution of 1909

The slow progress of irredentist programs, the growing social and economic problems, and the incompetence of the government enraged many Greeks including members of the media and especially members of the military. In 1908 a group of middle-rank and junior officers formed a para-military organization called *Stratiotikos Synthesmos* or Military League. On August 28, 1909, 3,000 officers and their men marched from Athens to Goudi on the outskirts of Athens and launched a coup known as the *Goudi revolt* or the *revolution of 1909*. The coup did not have any clear ideological or political content. It was an expression of discontent and anger against the dominant political factions and the monarchy (Tsoukalas, 1974, p. 14). The Military League was concerned with the "improper" promotion of officers who were in support of the Commander-in-Chief, Crown Prince Constantine. Furthermore, the League demanded national reforms similar to those introduced by the Young Turks whose movement supposedly the officers involved were imitating. The League required reorganization in administration, judiciary and education, the lowering of taxes, the strengthening of the armed forces, the removal of Prince Constantine and other members of the royal family from the armed forces because they had too much influence, the dismissal of the government, and the appointment of a new Prime Minister to carry out the aims of the revolution. In addition, the Military League wished their demands embodied in constitutional forms. The new Prime Minister, Mavromichalis, accepted the demands (Campbell & Sherrard, 1968, p. 110).

Mavromichalis being a nominal Prime Minister could not permit the leaders of the League from dominating government and to pass ill-considered bills including the abolition of the post of Commander-in-Chief and of the General Staff, and the dismissal of officers and government officials who did not support the young officers. "The anomalous character of this military influence," and the inability of the young officers to goals and objectives of reforming the political system and the army, had already cost the Military League some loss of respect and as a consequence it was decided to enlist the services of Eleftherios Venizelos. Venizelos had two important qualifications: he had opposed Prince George in 1906 when the latter had been High Commissioner in Crete and he was not committed to any of the political parties. Venizelos recommended that a National Assembly be elected to revise the constitution and the dissolution of the League be connected to the Assembly's convocation. The King, having no other choice, accepted the recommendations (Campbell & Sherrard, 1968, pp. 110-111). By March 1910, all political parties agreed to disband the *Stratiotikos Synthesmos*. The leaders of the League did not have much faith in any of the old politicians and by choosing Venizelos as their adviser they gave him the opportunity to become a national leader and Prime Minister of Greece. On October 18, 1910, King George, having failed to form a stable government, called upon Venizelos, the most charismatic politician of the first half of the twentieth century, to become the Prime Minister.

The divisive behavior of the political parties in the Assembly enabled Venizelos to create his own following and his own political party, the Liberal Party. He convinced the King to dissolve the Assembly and to call new elections. During the campaign, he promised to establish an honest administration and to create the conditions for national economic prosperity. Having created these conditions for a national revival, he said, the army would return to the barracks and its traditional duties. By this statement, he freed himself from the suspicion that he would be an instrument of the army. The people of Greece in January 1911 responded to his proposed program by electing 300 of 364 representatives to the Revisionist Assembly who were Venizelists. The large majority allowed him to pursue his legislative proposals with great intensity. "Among the revisions to the constitution of 1864 the inviolability of private property was qualified to permit the expropriation, with compensation, of large estates for the settlement of landless peasants. In order to prevent irresponsible obstruction by opposition parties, quorum of the chamber was reduced to one-third. Serving officers became ineligible as deputies. Established civil servants were entitled to security of tenure. Social legislation was introduced for employers' liability and for sickness and old age pensions. A bill was passed which prevented employers from interfering in the affairs of workers' organizations. A Ministry of Agriculture was established. Foreign advisers were introduced, particularly from Great Britain and France on whose influence and assistance Venizelos had already chosen to rely. With the appearance of political stability and this readiness to defer to foreign advice, and even control, capital flowed in from abroad to finance ambitious programs of public works and road construction. Although a number of the laws passed in this period were not immediately implemented, for instance in the field of social legislation or in the provisions for the redistribution of large estates, the promise of these measures had already at the time of the elections for the second Revisionary Assembly in December 1910 destroyed the independent threat of the Agrarians and Socialists whose support in a country with little industry and a population mainly consisting of peasant proprietors was local and limited even under favorable circumstances. With most sections of the community and particularly the urban bourgeoisie of merchants, entrepreneurs, and public servants, in general approval of the intentions embodied in Venizelos' first period of legislative and administrative effort, his Liberal Party won a second overwhelming victory at the elections for the normal parliamentary chamber held on 25 March 1912 in which it won 150 of the 181 seats" (Campbell & Sherrard, 1968, p. 112).

One of the greatest achievements of Venizelos was to convince the Greeks that through his reforms the country had been reborn. The Prime Minister was a national, not a social, revolutionary. He reformed the military. Many young officers who had been trained in France and Germany formed the nucleus of a professionally trained staff. He re-appointed to the military command Crown Prince Constantine, and he introduced military and naval missions from France and England to improve the organization of the two services. The state finances steadily improved, small-scale industry expanded, there was economic growth, the country's institutional structures improved; "but it is an exaggeration to suggest that on the eve of the Balkan wars in 1912 he had miraculously recreated the Greek state. The miracle consisted in the general belief that he had done so" (Campbell & Sherrard, 1968, pp. 113-114).

World War I

At this point in Greek history, Balkan nationalism flared into war, the First Balkan War, when the Balkan states of Montenegro, Serbia, Bulgaria, and Greece attacked the dying Ottoman Empire in October 1912. The Balkan states were so successful against the Ottomans; their victories compelled European powers to intervene. The English and French governments opposed the Greek desire to gain control of the Aegean islands and the Dardanelles. The Austrians were determined to prevent Serbia from gaining access to the Adriatic Sea and as a result they proposed the establishment of an independent Albania. The Russians did not wish the total destruction of the Ottoman Empire and did not want a rival power to gain control of Constantinople. The Bulgarians were near achieving that, control of Constantinople, having overrun Thrace. An attempt by Bulgaria to control the city would have caused a war with the Greeks, who considered Constantinople as their natural capital. Such a war was avoided when the Greeks captured Thessaloniki in November 1912, only a few hours before the Bulgarians. The Ottomans were persuaded to accept an armistice after the first two months of the war on December 3, 1912. It was signed in London, but the Greeks were not at the meeting. The war was not over even after the belligerents had decided on the terms of a peace treaty following intense negotiations in London. In January 1913, Enver Pasha, at the head of a group of Young Turks, overthrew the government that had signed the armistice, and renewed the war. Again, the war was disastrous. In May 1912 the Ottomans surrendered and the peace conference was resumed (Woodhouse, 1968, pp. 191-192).

The substantial territorial gains made by the Balkan states at the expense of the Ottoman Empire did not fully satisfy them. The Bulgarians disputed Greek possession of Thessaloniki. Furthermore, they disputed the possession of the rest of Macedonia by the Greeks and the Serbs. The Serbs were upset having lost access to the Adriatic Sea, and they along with the Greeks and the Montanegrins did not approve of the creation of Albania in 1913. The Greeks were content with the acquisition of Ioannina, Thessaloniki, and Crete, but they were deprived of northern Epirus, of a coastal strip of eastern Macedonia, and of a number of Aegean islands. In this very fluid and unpredictable environment the Greeks, the Serbs and the Romanians signed a treaty, and in a few months the Second Balkan War began against Bulgaria. Bulgaria lost the war and a treaty signed in Bucharest in August 1913 followed an armistice. Bulgaria lost territories to all her enemies but retained an outlet to the Aegean Sea. At the end of the two Balkan Wars, Greece succeeded in doubling its territories and increased its population from 2.7 to 4.4

million (Woodhouse, 1968, pp. 192-193). "The period 1909-13, especially the Balkan Wars (1912-13), represented a landmark in modern Greek history. . . . For the first time since independence, Greece had expended territorially as a result of its own efforts rather than through the good graces of the powers" (Couloumbis, et al., 1976, p. 35). Because of the Balkan Wars the military budget increased dramatically, and many members of the middle class entered the ranks of the military and were quickly promoted. As a consequence, the officers' corps lost its "aristocratic" character and became more like a pressure group interested in promoting the professional interests of its members. The transformation of the military, during a period of transition and weak civil society, made military intervention in politics inevitable (Mouzelis, 1987, p. 180), something that remained true until the mid-1970s. Yet the long history of military interference in Greek politics has led to only three dictatorships: the first imposed by Theodore Pangalos in 1925-1926, the second by Ioannis Metaxas in 1936-1941, and the third by Georgios Papadopoulos, Nikolaos Makarezos and Stylianos Pattakos in 1967-1974 (Maneses, 1987, pp. 11-12).

The accomplishments during the wars satisfied Greek national pride and "the dishonor of 1897 was redeemed" (Woodhouse, 1968, p. 193). Among those who greatly benefited was Crown Prince Constantine, who had been blamed for the 1897 calamity and who was deprived of his military rank by the *Stratiotikos Synthesoms* in 1909. Prince Constantine, as the Commander-in-Chief had played a significant in 1912-1913 in capturing Thessaloniki and Ioannina. But even before the Second Balkan War began, unfortunate events brought him to the throne as King Constantine I. King George I, while visiting the newly liberated Thessaloniki was assassinated by a mentally deranged man. The new king, who was Orthodox in faith and Greek by birth, was warmly welcomed. Having the same name as the last Byzantine Emperor, many hoped that he would fulfill the aspirations of the Greeks as related to the *Megali Idea*. Unfortunately for the new king, World War I broke out.

Despite friction in the past, there was an improvement, if only temporarily, in the relationship between Prime Minister Venizelos and King Constantine I because of the triumphs during the Balkan Wars and the circumstances of the succession. But this improved relationship was too good to be true. In the summer of 1914 Venizelos was on his way to Brussels to negotiate an agreement with the Ottomans when World War I started. Venizelos assured the Serbs, in case of an attack by Bulgaria,

Greece would come to Serbia's assistance. In addition, the Prime Minister made offers of support to the allies against Turkey as long as they guaranteed protection of Greece against Bulgarian attack. The allies did not accept the offer because at the moment they did not wish to expand the war and did not want to draw in Bulgaria or Turkey against them. Venizelos' overtures also were not acceptable to the King who was married to Sophia, the sister of the Kaiser, and was much impressed by Germany's military prowess (Woodhouse, 1968, pp. 194-195).

Ethnikos Dikhasmos

The first rift between the King and the Prime Minister materialized as soon as the war began. Prime Minister Venizelos convinced that the allies would win the war wished Greece to enter the war as soon as possible. He also argued that support of the allies would serve the interests of the *Megali Idea*. King Constantine did not agree with the Prime Minister and did not share his confidence in an allied victory. King Constantine believed that neutrality, knowing that he would not be able to persuade the people of Greece to join the Central Powers, would best serve the interests of Greece. The King knew that Germany had made the commitment to support Turkey and that Germany could not do anything for Greece. The alternative to neutrality was to wage war against powerful countries such as Germany, Austria and Turkey (Woodhouse, 1968, pp. 195-196). In rejecting the latter King Constantine had the support of the Chief of the General Staff, Colonel Ioannis Metaxas who later became Prime Minister and dictator (1936-1941).

There was strength to the arguments made by both the King and the Prime Minister. There was force to the King's position as long as Turkey and Bulgaria stayed out of the war. But Turkey joined the Central Powers on November 1914 and Bulgaria did the same a year later, and that, of course, caused a change in the relationship between the allies and Greece. While at first the allies were reluctant to respond to Greek overtures fearing the proliferation of the war, now they began to woo the Greeks. The Entente allowed Greece to occupy northern Epirus, promised territories in Asia Minor, and considered discussions over Cyprus. Prime Minister Venizelos, concerned with a Bulgarian attack, tried to secure Bulgaria's neutrality. When Bulgaria received loans from the Central Powers, which assured Bulgaria's participation in the war on their side, Venizelos sought commitments from the Entente. He wanted an Anglo-French force to land at Thessaloniki and wished Romanian intervention in case of an attack by Bulgaria. In return he promised that a Greek army corps would support the allied attack on the Dardanelles. Venizelos' plan was not easy to implement. The Romanians were not willing to participate, the Russians objected to the plan thinking that this might lead to Greek occupation of Constantinople, the English did not want to divert resources by sending troops to Thessaloniki and above all King Constantine had reservations (Woodhouse, 1968, 196-197).

When Venizelos attempted to secure the consent of King Constantine for Greece to participate in the Gallipoli campaign on the side of Entente, the two leaders disagreed so violently that the King dismissed the Prime Minister despite the large majority held in parliament by his Liberal Party. Venizelos was reelected the same year and was successful in persuading the King to allow English and French troops on Greek territory to protect Serbia. Allied troops landed in Thessaloniki. Shortly thereafter the King's sympathy toward Germany re-emerged and King Constantine forced the Prime Minister to resign over the same foreign policy issue for a second time the same year (1915). "The stage was set and the lights dimmed for the drama of the long struggle between the two men which was to plunge the monarchy and the 'constitutional question' of the king's powers into the political arena until they became the chief cause of dispute between political parties for many years and finally affected the whole of Greece's political life" (Carey & Carey, 1968, p. 93). The dispute between the two leaders is known as the *Ethnikos Dikhasmos* or National Schism. The division came at an unexpected time. As Veremis (1997) says: the Schism "came like a bolt from the blue" (p. 51). "The Schism destroyed consensus about the political system, and politicized the machinery of the state. Henceforth each of the camps had a military wing on which it depended for political power" (Close, 1995, p. 4).

Prime Minister Venizelos argued that the King had exceeded the powers afforded to him by the constitution. In accordance with the constitution of 1864 and its modifications in 1911, King Constantine was given a lifelong tenure and was to exercise only the powers conferred upon him by the constitution. But the constitution and the laws did not make it clear if the King, in the exercise of his right to appoint and dismiss ministers, had the power to dismiss a Prime Minister whose party had the majority in parliament and to do it twice during the same year. The King's actions gave the Entente as guaranteeing powers an excuse to intervene in the affairs of Greece and Venizelos a cause for making a revolutionary move. The conflict that resulted from these events continued for many years and ended with the coup d' etat of 1967.

In 1916, the allies seriously interfered in the domestic affairs of Greece. They demanded a new Greek government, the dissolution of parliament and demobilization of the Greek army. In October of the same year, Venizelos established a rival provisional government in Thessaloniki. Now Greece had two governments, one in Athens and the other in Thessaloniki. The allies flagrantly violated Greece's sovereignty by imposing a blockade against areas controlled by the royalists and by demanding the King's abdication (Clogg, 1992, pp. 92-93). Even though the King did not formally abdicate, he left Greece in 1917 and chose his second son, Alexander, to succeed him, and made it possible for Venizelos to return to Athens. The conflict between Constantine and Venizelos involved much of the Greek population. Venizelists who lived in areas under royal control were harassed, and purged from civil service and the government. The Archbishop of Athens pronounced an anathema on Venizelos and his supporters. When Venizelos returned to Athens as the Prime Minister of the entire country, the purges committed by the royalists were now matched or exceeded by the Venizelists themselves (Legg & Roberts, 1997, p. 35). Alexander's reign was brief (1917-1920) because of poisoning after being bitten by a pet monkey. After Alexander's younger brother, Paul, refused the throne, the Greeks were confronted with the options of recalling King Constantine, choosing another king, or abolishing the monarchy. In a plebiscite held in December 1920, the great majority of those who voted supported, probably as an attempt to demonstrate Greek independence from foreign powers, the return of Constantine. Amid great enthusiasm the King returned to Greece, but the allies were not pleased and withdrew their support from the country (Carey & Carey, 1968, p. 94). As Mourelos (1985) states "Contrary to what might appear at first glance, however, the Great Powers' policy in Greece should not be seen as a classical imperialist intervention in the limited Hellenic space. To be sure, the methods used by the Allies were imperialist in nature, having all the trappings of gunboat diplomacy (e.g., formulation of ultimatums, muscle flexing, blockade, military occupation of certain areas). Yet these tactics did not aim to secure future encroachment on the area so much as they tried to respond to the strategic needs of a given moment" (pp. 131-132).

The Treaty of Serves

The King and the Prime Minister were not destined to remain in power for very long. At the Paris Conference after World War I, Venizelos successfully represented the interests of Greece. He asked for northern Epirus, eastern Thrace, the Dodecanese islands, and Smyrna and the surrounding district. He also wanted to keep Constantinople under international control (Campbell & Sherrard, 1968, p. 123). All of Greece's claims found opposition with at least one of the allies. The President of the United States, Wilson, opposed the acquisition by Greece of Epirus and Thrace because the former would have involved partition of Albania, and the latter would have cut off Bulgaria from the sea. The Italians opposed Greek claims to Smyrna and the Dodecanese. The Italians had occupied the latter since 1911 and had been promised the former since 1916 (Woodhouse, 1968, p. 204). Nevertheless, the Treaty of Serves (signed on August 10, 1920) gave Greece eastern Thrace and all the Aegean islands, including Imbros and Tenedos, but excluding the Dodecanese, a number of which were to be demilitarized because they fell within the demilitarized zone of the Straits which included Gallipoli and either side of the Bosporos and the Dardanelles (Dakin, 1972, pp. 226-227). In addition, the Treaty of Serves gave Greece the administration of the Smyrna district, which was to remain under Turkish sovereignty for five years. At the end of the five-year period the people of Smyrna were to decide by a plebiscite if they would join Greece. Because of his success at the Paris Conference, Venizelos upon his return to Greece announced to parliament that Greece had expanded to "two continents" and "five seas" (Karolides, 1992, p. 172).

Even before the Treaty was signed, the Italians landed troops in southwest Turkey and began moving toward Smyrna. The movement alarmed England, France, and the United States so much as to allow Greece to send troops to Smyrna, and with allied support to occupy the city on May 15, 1919. The Treaty of Serves, which was never ratified, looked like the death certificate of the Ottoman Empire. But a new state was emerging from the ruins of the Empire: Turkey (Kleanthis, 1983, p. 36). The arrival of the Greeks revived Turkish nationalism under Mustafa Kemal (Ataturk-father of the Turks) and as the months passed his forces grew stronger. They were determined to recapture the territories in Asia Minor and eastern Thrace. "Unfortunately, Venizelos, not content with Greece's share, came to the opinion that it would be possible to form a great Greek province in Asia Minor" (Jelavich & Jelavich, 1965, p. 82). After his triumphant return from Paris Venizelos decided that the circumstances were politically favorable to call for new elections. The elections were held on November 14, 1920, and to his surprise his Liberal Party was soundly defeated and two days later went into voluntary exile. As Clogg (1992) states: "Defeat may have come as a surprise to virtually all observers but it was clear that the result reflected war weariness (the country had been on a war footing for the best part of eight years), coupled with feelings of resentment and humiliation at the meddling in the country's internal affairs by Britain and France and at the vengeful and arbitrary behavior of some of Venizelos' supporters during his second period in office between 1917 and 1920" (p. 95). As Prime Minister, Venizelos undertook harsh measures to protect himself from reactions by military and political opponents. He exiled politicians and military personnel, dismissed academicians and, in order to punish judges who had persecuted his supporters, he did not allow them to hold office for life (Vakalopoulos, 1987, p. 359).

The defeat of Venizelos permitted certain developments in the relations between Greece, Turkey, and the allied powers to take a more radical direction. The French wanted to prevent the return of the King and to modify the Treaty of Serves, which created a Greece close to the aspirations of those supporting the *Megali Idea* and closely allied to English interests. The English were not as strongly opposed to the King, but were more interested in saving the treaty. However, the English were concerned that King Constantine might not be as supportive of their interests in the eastern Mediterranean as Venizelos. The government of England decided to side with the French in a note delivered to the Greeks on December 3 stating that if the King was recalled the allies reserved the freedom to take any action necessary. Supporters of the King chose to think that the English would not withdraw their support and in a plebiscite the majority of the Greeks on December 5 voted for the return of King Constantine. Three days later the allies informed the Greek government that they would not continue their financial assistance. On December 19 King Constantine returned to Greece (Campbell & Sherrard, 1968, p. 125). Meanwhile, England, France, and Italy met in London (February-March 1921) to discuss modification of the Treaty of Serves in favor of Turkey.

Ethnike Catastrophe and the Treaty of Lausanne

The royalists, enchanted by the vision of a Greater Greece, changed their minds about the venture in Asia Minor and continued Venizelos' foreign policy. The Greek army was routed by Kemal's troops on September 8, 1922, and was forced to evacuate Smyrna. The defeat was so humiliating and had such long-term consequences; the Greeks refer to it as the *Ethnike Catastrophe* or National Catastrophe. The effort in Asia Minor failed for many reasons: First, the Greeks were fighting a war in a hostile environment that was far way from Greece. Second, the Greek economy was vulnerable to the pressures of warfare and the fluctuations of the world economy. Third, the government that resulted from the elections of November 1920 was a coalition government that was highly unstable; in two years there were six different governments. Fourth, even though the royalists campaigned on a peace platform they expanded the military effort once in power, thus intensifying war weariness. Fifth, Prime Minister Demitrios Gounares had little understanding of international relations. Sixth, the Ethnikos Dikhasmos had adversely affected the successful conduct of Greek foreign policy (Couloumbis, et al., 1976, pp. 44-45).

The Treaty of Lausanne signed on July 24, 1923, ceased the hostilities between Greece and Turkey and also wiped out the territorial gains made by Greece as a result of the Treaty of Serves. The Greeks lost to Turkey all the territories they had obtained in Asia Minor, eastern Thrace, and the islands of Imbros and Tenedos. Greece also lost to Italy Kastelorizo and the Dodecanese. The Treaty of Laussane ended the territorial designs of both Greece and Turkey, but did not create an environment of trust, which was necessary for the solution of the differences between the two countries (Veremis, 1992, p. 83). As a result of the *Ethnike Catastrophe* about 500,000 lost their lives. In addition, there was an exchange of populations, Turkey accepted 354,647 Muslims for whom there was an abundance of land and Greece had to deal with about 1,300,000 refugees, most of whom were destitute. "Thus in the hour of disaster, Greece, although her territory was reduced, achieved substantially her unification" (Dakin, 1972, p. 243). After the population exchanges, Greece emerged as ethnically homogeneous. Today there are near to 100,000 Muslims residing in Greece, and they are the only officially recognized minority. Furthermore, the Treaty of Laussane called for the revocation of the special guarantee, which England, France and

Russia had enjoyed by treaty since 1832 and used by them as a justification of intervention in the domestic affairs of Greece. The Asia Minor disaster signified the end of the *Megali Idea* as the dominant goal of Greek foreign policy. "Greece had to reconcile itself to a permanent status as a small state. In return, however, it liberated itself from a commitment whose implementation had occasioned foreign interference, caused internal dissention, and heavily over-taxed its scarce resources. For the first time, Greece had no alternative but to turn its attention inward toward internal development. Its sole obligation as a state was henceforth toward its citizens only, swollen as they were in number by the sudden massive influx of largely destitute refugees" (Couloumbis, et al., 1976, p. 45).

Many Greeks blamed Venizelos and the allies for the *Catastrophe*, and many others blamed King Constantine for the disaster even though it was not he who made the decision to go to war. After the debacle, a group of army officers headed by Nikolaos Plastiras looked for a scapegoat. They met on the island of Chios and from there they issued an ultimatum demanding that the King abdicates or they would march onto Athens and punish those responsible for the defeat. Although the King still maintained the loyalty of many in the military, he decided in favor of abdication. After the King's departure, a revolutionary council was established headed by Plastiras. A cabinet appointed by the council was instructed to govern until elections were held for a new parliament. The cabinet arrested, brought to trial, and sentenced to death former Prime Minister Gounares, four members of his cabinet and the commander of the Asia Minor army, Hadjianestis (Pantelouris, 1987, p. 71). During the trial, the ministers of England and Italy in Athens protested, and when the men were executed on November 1922, England broke off diplomatic relations with Greece. The tragic execution of the six men held responsible for the tragedy poisoned Greek political life until the collapse of the military dictatorship of 1967-1974. As Kousoulas (1973) says, "the chasm between the Venizelists and the Royalists turned into an abyss" (p. 16). For a generation after 1923, the debate in Greece was conducted in relationship to individuals and their followers rather than facts. There was, or was thought to be, a monarchist movement which became identified with the *Laikon Komma* or the Populist Party and an anti-monarchist movement identified with the *Phileleftheron Komma* or the Liberal Party. These two political parties were personified in two men: King Constantine and Venizelos. Their schism remained prevalent until another menace emerged on the horizon, that of communism (Woodhouse, 1968, pp. 212-213).

Before departing, King Constantine chose his eldest son, George, as his successor. The new King, George II, was a king in name only because real power was in the hands of the revolutionary council the key members of which were Nikolaos Plastiras, Stylianos Gonatas, and Theodoros Pangalos. The new King held the throne for just over a year before the institution of the monarchy once again became a source of friction. The most powerful members of the revolutionary council demanded the abolition of *Vasilevomene Demokratia* and the installment of a republic. King George II "was persuaded to leave for what was thought would be a short time to allow political passions to cool. They did not cool easily, however, and the king's exile lasted from 1924 until 1935" (Carey & Carey, 1968, p. 96). With the officers' support and confirmed by a plebiscite, the monarchy was abolished in 1924 and a republic was proclaimed. In February 1924, the parliament passed a resolution declaring that only a republican form of government would "put an end to the disastrous internal divisions" (Kousoulas, 1973, p. 17). The members of the royal family were deprived of their Greek nationality and their rights to the Greek throne. Yet "despite the constant arguments over the monarchy among the political parties, no strong tradition had grown up among the Greek people during their years of national life, nor had any serious preference for a republic appeared to be generally widespread" (Carey & Carey, 1968, p. 97).

The republic lasted for less than twelve years. Its history was uneasy and chaotic, with coups and counter-coups as well as years of constitutional government. From 1924 to 1935 the country underwent twenty-three changes of government, one dictatorship and thirteen coups of varying degrees (der Kriste, 1994, pp. 152-153). With the departure of King George II, Admiral Koundouriotis was elected President (See Table 3) and the new republican constitution was not formally put in place until 1927. A bicameral legislature was established with the Senate being the weaker of the two houses. In the interim, a group of higher officers launched a coup in 1926 and General Theodoros Pangalos, the chief of the army staff, established a military dictatorship (See Table 4), believing that it would end the political instability. He exiled political opponents, censored the press and stifled public opinion.

TABLE 3
Presidents of Greece Since 1924

P. Kountouriotis 1924-1926, 1926-1929
T. Pangalos 1926 (Dictator)
A. Zaimis 1929-1935
G. Papadopulos 1973 (Dictator)
Phaidon Ghizikis 1973-1974 (During Dictatorship)
M. Stasinopoulos 1974-1975
K. Tsatsos 1975-1980
K. Karamanlis 1980-1985, 1990-1995
Christos Sartzetakis 1985-1990
K. Stefanopoulos 1995-Present

Source: Data from Enoses Teos Voulefton (1985). *150 Chronia Hellenikes Demokratias*, p. 221. Athens: Helloekdotike.

TABLE 4
Dictators Since 1926

Theodoros Pangalos 1926
Ioannis Metaxas 1936-1941
Georgios Papadopoulos 1967-1973

Source: Data from Enoses Teos Voulefton (1985). *150 Chronia Hellenikes Demokratias*, p. 221. Athens: Helloekdotike.

Soon after coming to power, Pangalos stated that the constitution of the republic would be ready soon and it would strengthen the office of the president. The preparation of the constitution took much longer and at the same time the arrangements to have elections were incomplete and implemented only in a few districts. Pangalos was elected as President of the republic. Within a few days he was overthrown in a bloodless coup and was imprisoned. General Georgios Kondylis, the leader of the coup, was not interested in retaining power and wanted to reestablish the democratic process. New elections resulted in a coalition government consisting of monarchists and republicans. The public was tired of the military's involvement in politics and demanded a stable government. Little progress was made and the republic "tottered on shaky feet" (Carey & Carey, 1968, p. 99).

Parliamentary government received a new lease on life with the return of Eleftherios Venizelos in March 1928. Within a few months, as a result of the elections of August 19, 1928, he once again became the Prime Minister of Greece. His party gained 61.02 percent of the vote, the highest percentage by a center party until then. Although Venizelos was in power for more than four years and had strong majorities in parliament, he did not have much success on the domestic front. His presence sharpened political passions and caused and caused new divisions within the Greek political world. The strength of his party continued to decline and the democratic powers were so divided, they were not even in a position to agree to name a president to succeed Admiral Koundouriotis. Venizelos himself proposed Alexander Zaimis as candidate. Zaimis was elected and his victory led to temporary political stability. Abroad, Venizelos brought about dramatis re-orientation in Greek foreign policy "including reconciliation with Turkey and settlement of outstanding questions between Greece and Italy and Greece and Yugoslavia. But even his program in relation to Turkey brought him royalist opposition" (Carey & Carey, 1968, p. 100).

The return of parliamentary government failed to strengthen the republic. The role of government had expanded because of refugee settlements and the international economic depression, but the country did not have the capacity to cope with many of these problems. In the election of 1932, Venizelos and his party lost their majority; a coalition government was formed and it became necessary to call for new elections in 1933, which resulted in a victory by the Populist Party. A group of Venizelists officers, fearing that their interests were in danger, that they would be purged and that the republic was being undermined, attempted a coup under the leadership of General Nikolaos Plastiras. The 1933 coup failed in part because Venizelos himself did not support the effort. In 1935 there was a more serious attempt at military takeover. Officers occupied military installations, the cruiser Averoff and a few smaller ships joined the uprising, and Venizelos took part in the movement. It was a badly staged coup and the effort failed. Venizelos retired to the island of Rhodes and later Paris. As it turned out, the fears of the republicans were realized. Many were purged from civil service and the military, one of the officers was condemned by court-martial to death, and Venizelos and

Plastiras were also condemned to death in absentia. Foreign governments protested and called for reversal of the harsh decisions. But the army and navy were so deeply entrenched in the political life of Greece that the protests accomplished little (Carey & Carey, 1968, p. 101). It has been argued that the 1935 coup was the greatest mistake made by Venizelos who, along with Plastiras, conceived the idea of a coup. Democracy was fatally wounded (Vakalopoulos, 1987, p. 398) and Venizelos' political career had come to an end.

The ineffectiveness of republican governments and the resulting political instability did not mean that the republic did not have many supporters. In fact, the opposite was true. The royalists, however, gained the upper hand because republican groups decided not to participate in the elections of June 1935. Martial law was still in effect and the Populist Party emerged with an overwhelming majority in parliament. The Senate, dominated by republicans, was abolished. Prime Minister Panayis Tsaldaris refused to accommodate the demands of the monarchists for an immediate return of the King. Even though he also favored the King's return, he insisted that it must result from a fairly conducted referendum. Before the referendum was held the Prime Minister was forced to resign by a group of high-ranking officers (General Georgios Kondylis, General Alexander Papagos, Konstantinos Plates, and Georgios Reppas). The person behind the act was General Georgios Kondylis who happen to succeed Tsaldaris and who went ahead and abolished the republic. A farcical plebiscite was held on November 3, 1935, and 97.80 percent of the vote was in favor of the restoration of King George II. King George II attempted reconciliation by appointing Constantine Demertzis, a law professor and non-party man, to head a caretaker government until a new round of elections. General Ioannis Metaxas was his deputy and minister of war. The elections of 1936 produced even more deadlock because the monarchists won 143 seats, the republicans 141, with the communists holding the balance with 15 seats. When Prime Minister Demertzis died in April 1936, the King appointed General Metaxas, a royalist and the leader of a small right-wing party, as his successor. The major political parties, too preoccupied with their maneuvering, did not realize the danger in this and the parliamentary deadlock continued ('Athenian', 1972, p. 24).

Chapter 3

Ioannis Metaxas

Between January and May 1936 the death of four former Prime Ministers changed the political landscape in Greece: Kondylis (January), Venizelos (March), Demertzis (April) and Tsaldaris (May). Metaxas gave up on the idea of forming a parliamentary government and convinced King George II, who was alarmed by the political developments and the labor unrest, that constitutional monarchy was not possible and to consent to decrees dissolving parliament and to declaring martial law on August 4, 1936 (Heurtley, et al., 1965, p. 128). A dictatorship was instituted, known as the *Fourth of August Regime*, and the willingness of the King to go along with Metaxas was held against him. Metaxas announced that the dictatorship was an attempt to prevent the communists from seizing power. Others argue that the dictatorship was not the result of a communist threat or the deadlock created by the political parties; it was rather due to the fact that the political parties were about to agree to reinstate about 1,200 expelled Venizelist officers. The officer corps primarily consisted of royalists and the reinstatement of the Venizelists would have affected the royalist officers' prospects for promotion (Koliopoulos, 1977, pp. 38-48).

Metaxas wanted to change Greek society and refashion the Greek character based on Hitler's Third Reich. He thought of himself as the creator of a Third Hellenic civilization that would integrate the positive components of the Classical and Byzantine civilizations (Kourvetaris & Dobratz, 1987, p. 46). Metaxas' dictatorship lasted until his death in 1941 because of the apathy of the population, the disorganization of the opposing forces, and the support he received from the King. Metaxas owed his power to King George II, "who shared with him authority in the army, but otherwise valued the dictator for liberating him from politicians whom he had soon come to despise" (Close, 1995, p. 41). His domestic policy was incoherent, and his rhetoric included ethical statements, moderate socialist positions and totalitarian elements. He also demonstrated contempt for politicians and he detested communists. His government, however, improved transportation, introduced the eight-hour workday and minimum wages, and modernized the Greek army.

Metaxas expanded and centralized the state even more than previously. Most of local councils were dissolved and replaced by his appointees; he thoroughly censored the press; he carried further the trend toward corporative organization of the economy; and tried to regiment the population. His most well known effort to accomplish the latter was the creation, on the Nazi model, of the National Organization of Youth (EON), which became compulsory for all school children. The children received religious and patriotic instruction, and political indoctrination. Nevertheless, the four-year dictatorship of Metaxas was not as tyrannical as that of Mussolini or Hitler. There was no political freedom and he much depended on the police, but at the same time there were no political executions. Communists and other leftists were imprisoned or exiled, but not tortured. Freedom of expression was suppressed, but many Greeks did not have much difficulty making mockery of the dictatorship. Metaxas desired to create a modern state. For this reason he faced more opposition in the towns than the countryside. In the towns he was criticized for suppressing labor unions, for not freely debating and negotiating his social policies, and for thinking that the Greeks were incapable of effective administration under a democratic constitution. Towns' people believed that free institutions would not be abolished forever and that they would be restored with the collapse of the military regime (Woodhouse, 1968, p. 232).

At this moment in Greek history, the English government treated its relations with Greece in a businesslike manner. The form of government did not matter much as long as British interests were served. In addition, it was believed that as long as the King had the support of the army, the dictatorship might stabilize domestic conditions in Greece. Anglo-Greek relationship during the second half of the 1930s was unequal in nature, characteristic of a relationship between a great power and a small country. Even though Metaxas wanted a close alliance with England, the British preferred to only maintain a friendly relationship with Greece.

The nature of the relationship changed only because of the Italian attack on Greece (Koliopoulos, 1977, pp. 294-300).

Although the appeal of Metaxas' dictatorship was limited, he was tolerated because threats of war were present as a result of the actions of Mussolini and Hitler, and "the Greeks knew that it was not easy for them to combine political liberties with unity in the face of danger from authoritarian neighbors" (Carey & Carey, 1968, p. 123). During the early stages of World War II, Metaxas followed a policy of neutrality contrary to public opinion that was supportive of England and France. In 1940, after the fall of France and the declaration of war by Mussolini on the side of Germany, the Greeks began to prepare for war. The Italian government protested especially because of the willingness of the Greeks to allow the English to violate their neutrality. On August 5, 1940, Metaxas reaffirmed Greek neutrality. Mussolini reiterated his friendly intentions toward Greece as Italian aircraft attacked Greek ships at sea. On August 15, 1940, an Italian submarine sank the Greek cruiser Helle, which was in the harbor of the island of Tenos to attend the Feast of the Assumption. At the same time, Mussolini accused the Greeks for killing Daut Hodja, an Albanian.

Italian Invasion and German Occupation of Greece

Metaxas ordered mobilization of Greek armed forces in September 1940, but at the same time he pursued commercial negotiations with Germany and appealed to Hitler to restrain Mussolini. His efforts proved to be in vain because on October 28, 1940, the Italian Minister in Athens called on Metaxas to deliver an ultimatum as the Italian troops in Albania were crossing the frontier with Greece. Metaxas' response to the ultimatum was *Ochi* or No, which became the most famous response in Greek history since Leonidas at Thermopylae told the Persians to "Come and get it!" At that moment Greece became England's combatant ally. Even though the Greeks received some assistance from England, it was due to the Greek army, of which Metaxas was Commander-in-Chief and General Alexander Papagos as the Chief of Staff, that the Italian army was forced to withdraw. Initially the Greek forces were successful, but later on the course of the war turned against them. In January 1941, Metaxas died leaving Greece in less decisive hands (Heurley, et al., 1965, pp. 140-141).

It was now evident that Hitler would come to the rescue of Mussolini in the Balkans. In 1941, German troops began moving into Hungary, Romania and Bulgaria, with Yugoslavia willing to resist. The government of England, in anticipation of a German invasion, attempted to convince the Greek government to allow a British force to land in Greece. As long as Metaxas was alive, he wanted assurances that such a force would be sufficient to protect Greece. Initially the English government could not meet these requirements, having to meet an Italian threat in North Africa. The successor of Metaxas, Alexander Koryzis, insisted upon the same requirements. The successes against the Italians in North Africa led the government of England to conclude that it could now meet the requirements and to send high-ranking officials to Greece (including Anthony Eden, the Foreign Secretary, General Dill, the C.I.G.S., and General Wavell, the Commander-in-Chief of the Middle East). In March, the Greek government decided to accept the British force, which began to arrive in Piraeus. On April 6, the Germans attacked Greece and Yugoslavia, and the Balkan front began to disintegrate in a few days. On April 18 Prime Minister Koryzis committed suicide and the King appointed Emmanuel Tsouderos as Prime Minister. The dictatorship de facto came to an end. With the German forces in Greece, the King and the government escaped to Crete. On April 30 the Germans appointed General Tsolakoglou as Prime Minister. On May 20 they launched an attack on Crete and in ten days overran the island. The King and his government left for Cairo, Egypt, which at the time was under British domination (Heurley, et al., 1965, pp. 142-143). "Thus the King's government and armed forces fell under British control, while leaving their country leaderless to face its conquerors" (Close, 1995, p. 56). By June 1, 1941, Greece was under German domination, but the Germans never had effective control of the whole country. The Bulgarians were permitted to annex eastern Macedonia and western Thrace; the Italians were present in parts of Greece; and the Germans themselves were in charge of important communication routes. Greece, being a mountainous country with poor transportation and communications system, was left largely to itself and that meant starvation. It also meant the development of a resistance movement. During the German occupation (1941-1944) "the history of Greece divided into two streams, which flowed in their respective courses almost independently of each other" (Heurtley, et al., 1965, p. 144).

Greek Civil War

The Metaxas dictatorship was replaced by brutal foreign occupation first by Italy, and then Germany and Bulgaria; that, in turn, was followed by a fierce civil war, which lasted until the communists were defeated in 1949. In Greece, during the years of occupation there was a succession of governments willing to collaborate with the occupying forces. Outside of Greece, the Allies recognized the government-in-exile. Communication between those outside and inside in Greece was poor and the outcome was numerous misunderstandings, the most important of which was the failure of the government in exile to appreciate the strength of the anti-royalist sentiment in Greece. Many of the differences and misunderstandings remained hidden until then because of the war and the occupation. Resistance against the occupying forces began sporadically. In Athens, small groups appeared helping the people of Greece and later on were absorbed by larger organizations created by the Communist Party of Greece *(Kommunistikon Komma Ellados*-KKE). The Communist Party was the only group capable of activities against the occupiers. The National Liberation Front or the *Ethnikon Apeleftherotikon Metopon*-EAM, an umbrella political organization was created in 1941. The majority of those involved with EAM were not communists. The military operations were carried out by the National People's Liberation Army or *Ethnikos Laikos Apeleftherotikos Stratos*-ELAS. Even though communists were in control, some of the officers were republicans. Their primary goals were resistance to the occupation, and to influence the Greek government and society after liberation. The vision promoted by EAM/ELAS ignored the friction between republicans and monarchists, which appealed to many young people. Other non-communist resistance organizations did emerge, the most important of which was the National Democratic Greek League or the *Ethnikos Dimokratikos Ellinikos Syndesmos*-EDES. Both EAM/ELAS and EDES[1] very much opposed King George II for his acquiescence to the Metaxas dictatorship.

Outside of Greece, in the government-in-exile old differences re-emerged between the Populists and the Venizelists, which caused great upheaval. At that moment, two Liberals emerged as potential leaders: Georgios Papandreou, a follower of Eleftherios Venizelos, and Venizelos' son, Sophoklis. Papandreou became one of the most famous Greek leaders. In 1944, Prime Minister Tsouderos resigned and Sophoklis Venizelos was asked to form a government. Unable to do it, he resigned in a few days and Papandreou took the helm. In order to form a national unity government, Papandreou realized that he needed to invite to the conference not only representatives of political parties but also representatives of resistance groups, including communists. Because of the foreign occupation, the conference was held in Lebanon during May of the same year. It was agreed that the armed forces of the resistance movement and the government-in-exile would be under the command of Papandreou's government. A plebiscite would also be held to decide the return of King George II. The government-in-exile returned to Athens in October 1944 under British protection. While the government had about 10,000 troops, EAM/ELAS had approximately 40,000. A serious disagreement came to the surface when the government attempted to disarm EAM/ELAS and to gain control of the armed forces. A civil conflict ensued known as the *Dekemvriana,* which represented a significant point in Modern Greek history. The *Dekemvriana* determined that after World War II Greece would belong to the Western sphere of influence, and furthermore "marked an early stage in the Cold War. Indeed it proved to be the only occasion during the Cold War in Europe when the forces of a Western democracy fought against those of a Communist Party" (Close, 1995, p. 145).

The *Dekemvriana* involved Greek and British forces against units of EAM/ELAS. The armed clash began when on December 3, 1944, the police fired without prior warning at unarmed EAM/ELAS demonstrators, eventually killing about sixteen and wounding many others. The British intervened at that juncture in Greek history for two important reasons: first, they wanted the Greeks to have a "free choice" that might lead to democratic government; and second, and more important, the British wanted to keep the Russians out of the Mediterranean (Baerentzen & Close, 1993, p. 91). The British sent to Greece nearly 75,000 troops, which were assisted by the Greek National Guard. The conflict ended on February 15, 1945, with the *Varkiza* agreement and the defeat of EAM/ELAS. The ultimate outcome of the *Dekemvriana* was a result of the direct British military intervention. "The defeat of the Greek Communists in the streets of Athens showed that the classic concepts of proletarian revolution were no longer valid. With the development of modern weapons, the old form of popular revolution with the familiar features of street barricades, sharpshooters, revolutionary songs, and individual heroism is largely a thing of the past. There has been another, further transformation: to the traditional two protagonists in the class struggle, the 'proletariat' and the State, a third factor was added: foreign assistance to either of the two. In December 1944 the 'proletariat' in Greece launched its drive for the seizure of power while the 'State' was feebly armed and the middle segments of the people were neutralized in the iron grip of the 'proletarian' forces. According to the classic outlines of Leninist revolutionary theory, the Greek 'proletariat' should have won the battle, even with all the various tactical mistakes committed during the course of the conflict. But there was a third factor, which tipped the scales: the British military forces. By adding these forces to the side of the 'State', the 'proletariat' lost its original supremacy and, forced to face the overwhelming power of modern weapons, it suffered a crushing defeat" (Kousoulas, 1965, pp. 217-218).

The British persuaded King George II to step down in favor of Archbishop Damaskinos of Athens as regent and Papandreou was replaced as Prime Minister. Archbishop Damaskinos appointed General Plastiras, a well-known republican and head in absentia of EDES, to succeed Papandreou. It was agreed that EAM/ELAS would give up its arms, a plebiscite would decide the future of the monarchy and elections would be held for parliament (Jelavich & Jelavich, 1965, p. 119). The *Varkiza* agreement also provided for the restoration of civil liberties, the lifting of martial law, amnesty for political crimes committed during the *Dekemvriana,* the formation of a national army, and the purging from civil and security services of those who had collaborated with the occupiers during World War II (Alivizatos, 1995, pp. 157-158). The defeat of EAM/ELAS was a turning point in the fortunes of the Left, which had been successful against the Axis occupiers. In the liberated areas after the Second World War the communists had created a new social and political order. "Its structures differed radically from the traditional ones. The main features of the prewar state had been oligarchical rule, clientilism, 'rousfetism' and centralism. By contrast the new order was characterized by factors such as self-government, people's rights, voting, equality of women, decentralization to mention only a few. In brief, thanks to the Resistance Movement, a fundamental change of the Greek state was now within view" (Richter, 1980, p. 78).[2] But the subjugation of EAM/ELAS brought these changes to an end.

EAM/ELAS was defeated because it did not possess the means needed to continue the war. One of the greatest weaknesses of EAM/ELAS was its inability to avert widespread starvation especially in major cities such as Athens and Thessaloniki. People were in need of foreign aid. EAM/ELAS was also defeated because EAM authorities imposed higher taxes upon the wealthy, and in some instances people were killed for refusing to pay them, thus causing desertions in some places. Even in these circumstances, EAM/ELAS could have continued the fight if it had received support from communist parties in Albania, Yugoslavia, and Bulgaria. But they did not. By early February, EAM/ELAS leaders had realized that domestic and international public opinion was turning against them resulting from revelations of atrocities committed by their supporters during the fighting. According to American officers, members of EAM/ELAS sought to settle scores with opponents: members of EDES, gendarmes, and collaborators during the foreign occupation (Close, 1995, pp. 141-144).

From 1941 to the election of March 1946, Prime Ministers were virtually appointed by the British. After the *Varkiza* agreement the British refrained from conflict and began to train the Greek soldiers to do their own fighting, while reserving for themselves the right to act as the protectors of the Greek government. General Plastiras appointed old friends to positions in the army, the police, and the bureaucracy in order to change the composition of the security forces. But Plastiras was unsuccessful in dealing with the *ethnikophrosene* (the fiercely anticommunist and pro-monarchist) spirit that prevailed in the armed forces and the police. The *ethnikophrones,* unlike their opponents, were confident, were a cohesive group and with a strong sense of purpose. They were monarchists because they were Metaxists or because they believed that the monarchy was necessary to hold-off the communists. The prevalent ethos of the gendarmerie and the police was anticommunist. Those in the police and the gendarmerie who were in the resistance during the occupation were retired after the *Varkiza* agreement. Almost everywhere in the countryside, the police, the National Guard, and vigilante groups harassed and arrested members of the Communist Party and of EAM. Whatever limitations regarding prosecution of opponents found in the *Varkiza* agreement were merely ignored. By December more than 80,000 people were prosecuted and about 19,000 of these were in jail. A terror campaign was conducted by an alliance of army officers, members of the National Guard, armed thugs, and political organizations supported by people who were against EAM. At the time of and after the Varkiza agreement, the government was "a head without a body" (Close, 1993, p. 156). It was weak and had little, if any, support within Greece and had to depend on the anticommunist network, which was named by its opponents as the shadow state or the *parakratos* (Close, 1995, pp. 150-

156; Richter, 1980, p. 79). Behind the *parakratos* was a loose network of right-wing paramilitary organizations devoted to protecting Greece, with United States assistance, from the Left. While Greece was experiencing an economic "miracle," the country's cultural and intellectual life was held back by the phobias of the Right (Mazawer, 1993, p. 376). The "unofficial and official right-wing persecution of the Left ensured that peace would not return" (Pantelouris, 1987, p. 79). This behavior continued and in fact reached its apex during the years of the military dictatorship of 1967-1974. Only after the collapse of the dictatorship in 1974 steps began to be taken to approach the country's recent past more openly and to take necessary corrective actions. "Today, the services of EAM/ELAS fighters have been officially recognized by the state, and the old debates between Left and Right have lost much of their venom" (Mazawer, 1993, p. 376).

The *Varkiza* agreement, as mentioned earlier, provided for a plebiscite on the future of the monarchy to be followed by elections for parliament. The British and the Americans were under pressure to refute Soviet allegations that they themselves were subjecting Greece to occupation. They invited the Soviets to join them in observing the conduct of authorities during the plebiscite, an offer the Soviets refused. As a result of the actions of the *parakratos*, it soon became apparent that the chances of a fair plebiscite were not great. Consequently, the British, Archbishop Damaskinos and the Greek government decided that the plebiscite would polarize the country. The British and the Americans convinced the regent to appoint the 84 year-old Sophoules, a Venizelist, to head the government composed of members of the center, primarily of the Liberal Party, to create the necessary conditions for parliamentary elections. The election date was set for March 31 and an Allied Mission for Observing the Greek Elections (AMFOGE) consisting of over 1,200 British, American and French representatives arrived in Greece in February to prepare for the elections (Close, 1995, pp. 173-174).

The members of AMFOGE and the government of Sophoules could do nothing to prevent the coercion of voters and the distortion of the electoral results by the *parakratos*. The election was held on March 31, 1946, with the Populist Party receiving 156 seats and its monarchist allies 80, out of 354 parliamentary seats. The National Political Union won 68 seats and the Liberal Party, the only solidly republican party, received only 48. Approximately 49 percent of the electorate voted because many people were still refugees, others were afraid to vote, and the communists refused to participate. The primary purpose of the election was not to give the public an opportunity to express its opinion, but rather for the newly elected members of parliament to decide the future of the monarchy. It was clear that the majority of them wished the return of King George II (Carey & Carey, 1968, p. 140).

The plebiscite was held on September 1, 1946, with 1,666,511 out of 1,861,145 registered voters cast their ballot in favor of the King's return. The plebiscite did indicate, however, who among the voters would have preferred no King at all, who opposed the King's return because of his actions during the Metaxas dictatorship, or how many republicans voted for his return just because they feared that communism would be the alternative (Carey & Carey, 1968, p. 141). After the plebiscite, Archbishop Damaskinos resigned and King George II returned to Greece at the end of September 1946. But the King was not destined to remain in power for long. Seven months after his return he died and was succeeded by his younger brother, Paul. King Paul I began his reign during one of the darkest periods in Modern Greek history. The success of the Right, the terrorist acts of the *parakratos* against the Left with British encouragement, the unwillingness of the Right to compromise and the Greek Communist Party's policies provoked the Greek Civil War of 1946-1949 (Kofas, 1989, p. 2).

End of British Interference and the Beginning of United States Involvement

The Communists in Greece received not only encouragement from their communist brethren in Albania, Bulgaria and Yugoslavia, but they were also provided with weapons and supplies, which made possible the creation of a new guerrilla army, the "Democratic Army," under the strict control of the Communist Party. It is clear that without the support of the other Balkan communist parties, and especially Tito's, the Greek Civil War would not have developed into anything more than sporadic guerrilla attacks. Although the ultimate success depended on Stalin's actions, Stalin elected to be cautious and was not interested in provoking the United States over Greece while attempting to consolidate his control of Eastern Europe. The Soviets pursued a two-front strategy, at least from 1945 to 1946. In the near term, they wanted the Communist Party of Greece to coexist with a weak government in Athens, which itself would remain within the Western sphere of influence. The objective was to create a "soft" state, allied with the West, with strong communist presence that would prevent anti-Soviet policies. In the long term, the Soviet government was interested in creating the conditions that would allow for a more aggressive military policy. This Soviet strategy failed because by the end of 1946 political rivalries in Greece led to a civil war (Stavrakis, 1995, p. 228). By 1948 Stalin had concluded that all was a mistake: "they have no prospect of success at all. What, do you think that Great Britain and the United States—the United States, the most powerful state in the world—will permit you to break their line of communication in the Mediterranean? Nonsense . . . The uprising . . . must be stopped, and as quickly as possible" (Dunbabin, 1994, pp. 72-73). Stalin's difficulties with Tito and the expulsion of Yugoslavia from Cominform in 1948 even more complicated how the Soviets dealt with the crisis in Greece. Tito encouraged the activities of the Greek communists because he was competing with the Soviets for influence over the communist parties in Greece, Albania, and Bulgaria (Banac, 1995, p. 259). Although the Greek communists sought and received support from abroad, they launched their insurrection on their own. The Greek crisis of 1946-1949 was domestically conceived and that is why the communists labeled the insurgency the people's revolution or *laiki epanastasi* (Iatrides, 1995, p. 5).

Churchill's defeat in 1945 did not change British policy toward Greece and the Labour government that followed continued to assist Greek politicians as long as they were anticommunists. From 1945 to 1946, the British government supplied the Greeks with financial, military and technical assistance. It played a crucial role in determining the timing of elections in Greece, and trained the Greek armed forces and the police. "Then, suddenly, in late 1946, realizing that propping up Greece was a task Britain could no longer afford to perform alone, the cash-poor Attlee government sought to involve a far more powerful partner" (Iatrides & Rizopoulos, 2000, p. 98). As Papandreou (1974) says: "In February 1947 Great Britain recognized the bankruptcy of its policy in Greece and its inability to afford the cost of 'saving democracy in Greece'" (p. 100). Until then and since the period of the Balkan Wars, Greece was almost completely attached, militarily and diplomatically, to Britain (Couloumbis, 1978, p. 17). The United States government's views regarding the Greek Civil War were changing incrementally. Even a year after the *Varkiza* agreement, the United States embassy kept dismissing reports that the

Greek communists were Soviet tools. Instead, Ambassador MacVeagh said that the government in Athens resembled a Fascist government and that its actions against the communists would bring an alliance between democrats and communists, which would have resulted in the same kind of an ideological war as the one in Spain (Iatrides & Rizopoulos, 2000, p. 98). But quickly thereafter views about the situation in Greece began to change, change that was reflected in the tenor of reports regarding circumstances in Greece. On March 11, 1946, as George Kennan's "Long Telegram" was being circulated, a State Department memorandum stated that Greece was in the Soviet plans for expansion into the Middle East, the Mediterranean, and the Indian ocean. It was also stated that Greece and Turkey were two democratic countries that had an opportunity to present a strong front in halting Soviet expansion. The dramatic change in policy toward Greece coincided with other international developments that alarmed officials in the United States. The United States government now began to more fully implement its containment policy. It could be argued that the containment policy was first applied in Greece and Turkey.

The Truman Doctrine and the Marshall Plan

The United States became politically, economically, and ideologically involved in Greece. On March 12, 1947, President Truman gave a speech before a joint session of Congress and announced what has become known as the Truman Doctrine. He said: "At the present moment in world history nearly every nation must choose between alternative ways of life. The choice is too often not a free one. One way of life is based upon the will of the majority, and is distinguished by free institutions, representative government, free elections, guarantees of individual liberty, freedom of speech and religion, and freedom from political oppression. The second way of life is based on the will of a minority forcibly imposed upon the majority. It relies upon terror and oppression, a controlled press and radio, fixed elections, and the suppression of personal freedoms. I believe that it must be the policy of the United States to support free peoples who are resisting attempted subjugation by armed minorities or by outside pressures. I believe that we must assist free peoples to work out their own destinies in their own way" (Merrill & Paterson, 2000, p. 221). Despite the democratic values expressed in the

Truman Doctrine, it was the geographic location of both countries that was more important to the United States than the character of their government (Hook & Spanier, 2000, p. 51). Greece, as well as Turkey, has had the misfortune to be one of the most strategically located countries in Europe (Stavrianos, 1952, p. 3). Presidential aide Clark Clifford called the Truman Doctrine "the opening gun in a campaign to bring the people up to the realization that the war isn't over by any means" (Paterson, Clifford & Hagan, 2000, p. 241).

President Truman asked Congress to appropriate $400 million for Greece and Turkey in order for the two countries to remain free, with $100 million going to the latter while $300 million went to the former. The Truman Doctrine "represented the first link in a 'chain of steel' that the West placed around Soviet communism in order to contain it" (Goldstein, 1984, p. 15). The government of the United States was determined to defeat the communists and any political settlement was out of the question. American "penetration" was much more extensive than under the British, and even though Greek sovereignty was seriously undermined; United States involvement was welcomed by most of the anticommunist elite (Iatrides & Rizopoulos, 2000, pp. 99-100). In addition, on June 6, 1947, the United States Secretary of State, George C. Marshall, delivered a speech to the graduating class at Harvard University, which initiated the Marshall Plan or European Recovery Program, ERP. The Marshall Plan, through which the United States committed $13 billion to European reconstruction, was an extension of the Truman Doctrine and a prelude to the North Atlantic Treaty Organization (NATO). The Marshall Plan was designed as a reconstruction program for Europe, but it also served the geopolitical, strategic, and economic interests of the United States (Kofas, 1989, pp. 107-109). The Marshall Plan did not contain any references to the Soviet Union and communism, and the Secretary of State opened the program to all European countries. He knew, however, that the Soviet Union would not allow its allies in Eastern Europe to ask for aid (Schulzinger, 1990, p. 209).

In essence, the Truman Doctrine and the Marshall Plan guaranteed the security of Greece against communist threat. This was a development of great significance because the United States became involved in the struggle for control of the Balkans, and "in a sense, therefore, America stepped into Britain's shoes, emerging as the historic successor to British Balkan diplomacy and military action during the nineteenth century" (Brown, 1992, p. 6). In addition, the United States, as the founder of

NATO, shaped the post World War II security system and created the conditions for Western European countries to experiment with economic and political integration (Stavrou, 1999, p. 188). The Truman Doctrine and the Marshall Plan were widely applied in Greece and helped the government to defeat the communists. The communists were also defeated because the Soviet Union and the Balkan communist states, especially Yugoslavia, decided to discontinue their support of the rebels. By 1952 Greece had received nearly $1 billion from the United States. As a consequence of the Truman Doctrine and the Marshall Plan, Greece became dependent upon the United States. The state of dependency allowed the United States to play a primary role in Greek foreign policy as well as Greek domestic affairs. As Couloumbis (1993) asserts, "Greek Governments in the 1947-55 period faced a condition of structural dependency vis-à-vis the United States that could be referred to as a patron-client relationship" (p. 381).

The consequences of the United States intervention in the Greek Civil War were profound and enduring. On the positive side, the communist forces were defeated and as a result Greece did not experience an eastern European style communist dictatorship. Furthermore, because of NATO membership, secured in 1952, and the European Recovery Program, Greece benefited from the additional security and underwent a remarkable economic recovery. On the negative side, the Greek Right was ready for even more revenge and made little effort for reconciliation and to correct the many class disparities that made the communists so popular not long before the Civil War.

As for the United States, the consequences were also important. From 1947 to 1949, the United States had four main objectives in Greece: First, to create a government that would have the support of the majority of the Greeks; second, to make the state bureaucracy efficient and capable of addressing the needs of the people; third, to provide the necessary economic and technical assistance for Greece to enter a period of stability and prosperity; and fourth, to reorganize the armed forces in order to totally defeat the communists. The outcome of these policies was mixed. On the one hand, American assistance strengthened the Greek armed forces to such an extent to enable them to defeat the communists in two years. On the other hand, the United States policy in Greece during the war was interventionist and often insensitive. The American emphasis on achieving short-term goals made it difficult for the Greeks to find solutions to longstanding problems (Iatrides & Rizopoulos, 2000, pp. 100-101).

Right-Wing Dominance

From 1947 to 1949 Greece was governed by coalition governments. These governments "turned out to be less than unified, less than national, and far from lasting" (Carey & Carey, 1968, p. 147). The challenges, of course, were staggering and became necessary to impose martial law, which was not lifted until the end of the Civil War. The war of independence in the early nineteenth century and the National Schism during World War I caused important cleavages in Greek society. But these divisions could not compare with the savagery of the Civil War, which prolonged the agonies of the World War II occupation. The old conflict had been between Venizelists and anti-Venizelists, generally speaking between republicans and monarchists, but this schism had now been enhanced by an even more important division, that between communists and anti-communists (Clogg, 1992, p. 145).

The Civil War was costly not only in terms of people and money, but also because it delayed reconstruction after the end of World War II. The outcome of the struggle was high inflation, serious economic depression and a cost of living that was so high 1.5 million people were near starvation. At the end of the Civil War, the Greek government was directly assisting nearly 34 percent of the people either through government employment, pensions and refugee relief (Legg & Roberts, 1997, p. 45). "Perhaps more important in the long term, the military as an institution acquired the position of national savior and remained a major drain on the national budget (with military and security personnel numbering nearly 250,000) as well as a significant political player. Perhaps even more significant, the defeat of the communists also meant that the moderate Left lost its opportunity to be a legitimate participant in parliamentary politics. The possibility of forming a political party with a mass base and a modern agenda was delayed for a generation" (Legg & Roberts, 1997, p. 45).

With peace re-established, the people of Greece and the ruling class wished for tranquillity and political stability. It was agreed to call for new elections in April of 1950 with the understanding that no political leader will begin campaigning before the decision to have elections was announced. What followed was a nightmare rather than political stability because of the large number of governments formed between 1950 and 1952. The political instability convinced General Alexander Papagos to resign from the military and to enter politics. Old political leaders did their best to prevent him from entering politics believing that he would defeat them (Gregoriades, 1975, Vol. 4, pp. 9-19). In the elections of November 16, 1952, his right-wing party (Greek Rally) won 247 seats in parliament out of 300, an electoral outcome that satisfied the United States government (Benetatos, 1977, p. 99). The year 1952 initiated a new era in Greek politics characterized by stability unparalleled since the beginning of the Modern Greek state. From 1952 to 1963, Greece had only two prime ministers (General Papagos and his successor Constantine Karamanlis), in contrast to the pre-1952 period when half a dozen governments a year was not out of the ordinary. The government was in the hands of the conservative party (Greek Rally), and when the conservative government fell in 1963, another party replaced it after a constitutionally conducted election-a rare occurrence in Europe, outside of Great Britain, since 1945 (Woodhouse, 1968, p. 265).

The day before Papagos' funeral (1955), King Paul invited Karamanlis to form a new government. The King also gave him the authority to dissolve parliament and to call for new elections. King Paul had decided to bypass two deputy Prime Ministers (Stefanopoulos and Kanellopoulos) with much more experience. Karamanlis was one of the most popular members of the Papagos' government. As the Minister of Public Works he demonstrated determination and ability to push through projects that had been gathering dust for a long time. Of the two deputy Prime Ministers, Kanellopoulos, whose niece was married to Karamanlis, agreed to help. The other, Stefanopoulos, left the party and took with him twenty-nine Rally deputies. Karamanlis' sudden ascent led to rumors that he had been chosen by the palace, the United States government and the British. In 1956, Karamanlis decided to end the Greek Rally and to create a new party, the National Radical Union or ERE. By doing so, Karamanlis wanted to underscore the fact that he was a leader on his own right (Kousoulas, 1974, pp. 137-139). Karamanlis governed Greece for eight years (1955-1963). Even though the traditional political parties of Greece emerged intact from the Civil War, it was the Right, which was the beneficiary of the defeat of the Left. The Communist Party of Greece was outlawed, the electorate became polarized, and, above all, the emergency legislation, which laid the foundations for the paraconstitution and for the institutionalization of the anticommunist state in Greece, was put forward (Diamantouros, 1991, p. 144). Anticommunism became the ideology of powerful ruling groups (Ioakimidis, 1984, p. 35), and arrangements were made to neutralize the Left and to ensure the political dominance of the Right (Diamantouros, 1991, p. 16). The Right, viewed as the victor after the Civil War, created a system that systematically excluded from power all the forces on the "losing" side. This exclusivist system, which began to develop after World War II, was solidified by 1952. Furthermore, this system, other than outlawing the Communist Party and persecuting its supporters, it revived the patron/client network to promote the interests of the conservatives, it re-established state control of syndicalistic movements, and it maintained a large army (Mouzelis, 1987, pp. 237-240).

During the years of stability Greece became a member of the United Nations, NATO, and eventually (by a treaty of association) the European Economic Community (EEC). The relative tranquility of the Greek political life was shaken by the uneven economic development, the renewal of violence in Cyprus, especially in 1964, and the crisis in defense policy, which caused the collapse of the government and shook the monarchy in 1965 (Woodhouse, 1968, pp. 285-286). In the 1950s, Greece chose the path of full integration into the international economic community and of rapid growth. In spite of the impressive economic development, the average rate of growth was about 6 percent; there were serious structural problems. Economic growth did not increase employment opportunities and wages remained stagnant. The social dislocation caused by the rapid growth exacerbated the inequalities within the industrial labor force and the lower middle class. The resulting discontent became evident during the 1950s, but it took center stage in the early 1960s as demonstrated by the victory of the Center Union Party in 1963 and 1964. The victory of the center forces signified that the exclusivist political system in Greece had to change. Changes, however, were bound to affect the balance-of-power among the major players within the political system (Diamantouros, 1991, pp. 144-145). As Mouzelis (1978) states: "The balance had to tilt on the side of liberalism (opening-up of the system to the masses), or on the side of repression. The colonels and those who were behind them decided on the latter solution; setting themselves against rising pressures for broader political participation (a concomitant of capitalist growth), they had to establish a repressive apparatus much more complex and far-reaching than anything experienced during the inter-war period (p. 112).

The exclusivist state was undermined not only by the economic inequalities caused by the rapid industrialization, but also by the massive rural exodus. During the 1950s and 1960s, about 1.5 million people out of a population of 9 million left the countryside. Many found jobs in the cities, others, who were not successful in finding employment, immigrated to Western countries. These developments helped the Greek economy, but simultaneously disturbed family relationships. Additionally, the unfolding events expanded the intellectual horizons of the Greeks, which in turn made the existing social inequalities more obvious (Mouzelis 1987, p. 240).

In the mid-1950s, opposition parties began to increase their syndicalist activities. More specifically, in 1956, the Left established the Democratic Syndicalist movement and the Democratic Syndicalist Change, which organized labor organizations close to center forces. The numerous strikes that followed demonstrated the level of popular mobilization, which weakened the Right and strengthened the opposition. In the 1958 elections, the Left became the main opposition party after having won 24.4 percent of the popular vote. The student movement became more intense and fierce especially in 1960, and the Left was instrumental in accomplishing that. All of these happenings alarmed the repressive state apparatus, especially strong anti-communist officers in the army and the Central Service of Information (KYP). These officers desired to neutralize the communists and to influence the outcome of the 1961 election. The 1961 election denoted an important turn in the political developments of Greece because the Right decided to suppress not only the Left but also the Center. The blind attack against all opposition constituted the beginning of *Anendotos*, the famous campaign of George Papandreou against the exclusivist state (Mouzelis, 1987, pp. 241-242).

Under the existing conditions, George Papandreou and Sophoklis Venizelos in September 1961 united the center forces, until then divided, under the umbrella of the Center Union Party. They accused Karamanlis and his government of committing fraud in the elections of 1961. It seems that there was ballot manipulation and ERE received 2-4 percent more votes than it should have ('Athenian', 1972, p. 42). The assassination of Grigorios Lambrakis, a leftist member of parliament, in 1963 by an extreme right-wing organization with close connections to the police worsened Karamanlis' position. The monarchy began to promote the idea of a Center Union government because Karamanlis had become too independent and his position had been compromised by the assassination of Lambrakis. Karamanlis resigned on May 18, 1963, and went into a self-imposed exile in France during the next eleven years, not to return until he was called back to Greece after the fall of the junta in 1974.

The Center Union won the elections of November 1963, but did not gain a majority in parliament. To govern, Papandreou had to rely for support on the Right or the Left. However, his campaign was based on "the battle on two fronts, against both authoritarianism of the right and totalitarianism on the left" ('Athenian,' 1972, p. 43). Papandreou had no alternative but to ask the King, which he did, to call for new elections. "Papandreou naturally welcomed this chance to achieve an overall majority in parliament, particularly since his most redoubtable opponent on the right, Karamanlis, had withdrawn from the fray" (Clogg, 1987, p. 47). A few months later, in the elections of February 1964, George Papandreou (Sophoklis Venizelos died the same month) triumphed by winning 53 percent of the vote. "The outcome of the election of 1964 was an unpleasant surprise and a 'dangerous sign' for the Right, which had been accustomed for the past thirty years to being in power" (Stasinopoulos, 1985, p. 149).

In 1964, there was a crisis in Cyprus, the result of the unworkable constitution, which was the child of the Zurich-London agreements of 1959. President Makarios of Cyprus announced his decision to unilaterally revise the constitution in 1963 because it allowed the Turkish Cypriots to frustrate the administration of Cyprus. The Greek Cypriots were not pleased with the ability of the Turkish Cypriot minority to paralyze the Cypriot government by using its veto power granted by the 1960 constitution. Violence between the Greek and Turkish Cypriots broke out, and an uneasy peace returned with the arrival of the United Nations Peace Keeping force (UNFICYP) in 1964 (Kaloudis, 1991, p. 30). In the 1960s, the United States attempted to prevent the escalation of the Cyprus conflict fearing that a war over Cyprus between Greece and Turkey would endanger NATO. Negotiations were held between the two communities, but "since the Greeks persisted in believing that the basis of negotiations was *enosis* for Cyprus, coupled with compensations for Turkey, it was not surprising that they proved abortive" (Woodhouse, 1968, p. 287).

The Cyprus crisis proved to be a serious problem for Papandreou's government. Western powers, especially the United States, wished for the Greek government to reach what the Greeks viewed an unacceptable compromise. Papandreou, who had previously criticized Karamanlis for making too many concessions to the Turks, resisted. That, of course, did not make him popular with the American government, and some opposition leaders began to suggest to the Americans that a right-wing government would be more flexible. Papandreou came to power in early 1964 as hostilities between the two Cypriot communities were reaching a climax. He preferred to pursue a political settlement through the United Nations-a move that the United States opposed. His objective was to secure at a minimum an independent and unitary status for Cyprus, and at a maximum to work toward *enosis*. Papandreou's Cyprus policies were different from those of the United States. The American government wished for a settlement within the NATO alliance and away from public forums such as the United Nations. The American government advocated the adoption of the Acheson Plan, which called for the partition of Cyprus. More specifically, the Acheson Plan called for: Cyprus to unite with Greece; cession of the Greek island of Kastellorizo to Turkey; the establishment of a Turkish military base in Cyprus; the creation of two cantons under Turkish Cypriot administration, so they could have a degree of autonomy; and payment of compensation to Turkish Cypriots who wished to emigrate to mainland Turkey (The Christian Science Monitor, 1 August 1964, p. 5). The Turkish government accepted the plan as a basis for negotiations, but insisted that the base should be large enough for all Turkish Cypriots to live there. Both Papandreou and Makarios opposed the Acheson Plan and the stage was set for a confrontation between the Papandreou government and the Johnson administration (Couloumbis, et al., 1976. pp. 131-133). Mr. Clerides, President of the Cypriot House of Representatives, stated that acceptance of the plan "would have meant a betrayal of the whole of Hellenium" (*Keesing's* 14 no. 2 (5-12 Septmber 1964): 20269).

Following World War II, the vital interests of the United States in Greece could be summarized as follows: maintaining American and NATO bases; maintaining unrestricted military transit and over-flight rights over Greek territory; maintaining a friendly relationship between Greece and Turkey in order not to disturb the NATO alliance; and to maintain a friendly economic climate in Greece for American investors. In pursuing these interests, the United States government chose for the most part to champion conservative and anticommunist parties. It was only during the early 1960s when the American government briefly flirted with the idea of supporting the Center Union Party of George Papandreou. More precisely, during the difficult period of 1965-1967, the American government tilted in favor of King Constantine and against the government of George Papandreou. Many allegations have been made regarding the role of the United States including subsidizing the breakup of the center forces and the walkout of the so-called *apostates* from the Center Union Party (Couloumbis, et al., 1976, pp. 133-134).

Ultimately, what led to the fall of Papandreou's government and the dispute with the King was control of the armed forces, of which the King was the Commander-in-Chief. By the end of the Greek Civil War, a group of strongly anticommunist officers who while in Egypt in 1944 created the secret organization *IDEA* (Sacred Bond of Greek Officers), had a powerful influence within the army. For individuals to join *IDEA* they had to have the recommendation of two *IDEA* members, they had to be fiercely anticommunist, they had to be supporters of the monarchy and an opponent of the Liberal Party. Members of *IDEA* did everything possible to prevent the return of liberal officers who had been removed from the military service and to preserve the anti-Communist climate through out the country. According to Karagiorgas (1975) the members of *IDEA* not only wanted to control key positions in the military, they also wanted their members upon retirement to occupy important political offices (3). In 1958, a group of *IDEA* officers, led by the future dictator Georgios Papadopoulos who had joined *IDEA* in 1947, created a sub-group named *EENA* (Union of Young Greek Officers), which played a role in the 1961 elections. The members of *EENA* labeled themselves as *ethnikophrones* and wished to eliminate from the armed forces all republicans and those considered communists (Danopoulos & Gerston, 1990, p. 531). The group invented a plan called *'Pericles'* to influence, in favor of ERE, the vote of military personnel as well as of people in the provinces (Chondrokoukes, 1974, pp. 27-28).

Even though Prime Minister Papandreou was cognizant of the danger presented by *IDEA*, he did not effectively deal with the challenge confronting him. He could have taken a strong stance against the officers at the risk of military intervention, or he could have compromised in an attempt to avert aggravating military officers. Papandreou chose to follow a middle of the road path, which did not neutralize the officers and did not prevent them from continuing their activities (Gregoriades, 1975, Vol. 4, p. 373). Papadopoulos and some of his close associates were removed from important positions within KYP and were either sent to border military units or to Cyprus. Members of *IDEA* retaliated by creating an atmosphere of anticommunist hysteria. For example, Papadopoulos in 1965 announced the discovery of a communist conspiracy within a military unit in northern Greece. It was determined that there was no such conspiracy. However, Papadopoulos was not punished.

An earnest anticommunist campaign began in May 1965 when a small group of officers opposed to *IDEA* were accused of creating in 1964 a leftist para-military organization within army named *ASPIDA* or 'Shield' (also an acronym for 'Officers, Save Fatherland, Ideals, Democracy and Meritocracy'). Supposedly, the leader was Andreas Papandreou, the son of the Prime Minister. It is true that such an organization was established in Cyprus, but as discovered later, it was not significant. Some argue that the members of *ASPIDA* just wanted to promote their professional interests, while others say that the officers involved were against the use of the army as a tool by the anticommunist Right (Zacharopoulos, 1976, p. 67). Additionally, the extent of the involvement of Andreas Papandreou was not clear. Nonetheless, the *ASPIDA* affair dominated political developments and caused a serious conflict between King Constantine, who had succeeded his father King Paul in 1964, and George Papandreou. The King was convinced that the two Papandreous were conspiring to control the army and ultimately the Crown itself. King Constantine believed that the support of the army was essential for the survival of the monarchy, "for he had been told many times by his late father to safeguard its loyalty as the apple of his eye" (Kousoulas, 1973, p. 34).

Prime Minister Papandreou, convinced that his government was being undermined by the developments within the army, dismissed the Minister of Defense and sought to assume the post himself. Garouphalias, the Minister of Defense and a friend of the royal family, frustrated Papandreou's efforts to bring officers in whom he had confidence and who were supportive of him. The King, who was much influenced by his unpopular mother Queen Frederica, accepted the dismissal of the Defense Minister, but did not appoint Papandreou to take his place. Queen Frederica was a domineering person with a group of reactionary advisers. She was anti-democratic and according to some anti-Greek (Pettifer, 1993, p. 21). Papandreou offered his resignation believing that the king would either appoint him or dissolve parliament. "Instead, the King dismissed him and set about forming a new government from the existing parliament. It was a bold move with damaging consequences" (Woodhouse, 1968, p. 288). While the Left continued to remain on the periphery as a result of the restrictions imposed upon it, the forces of the center demanded greater democratization of the Greek political system and a more equitable distribution of wealth. The establishment refused to do anything and the ensuing conflict caused further erosion of the legitimacy of the political system.

The political instability was abundantly clear. From 1963 to 1966, the average life span of each government was six months, and from 1965 to 1967, five caretaker governments ruled Greece (Blais & Dion, 1990, p. 260). The first four governments, composed of members of different political parties including *apostates* or defectors from the Center Union, were headed by Novas, Tsirimokos, Stephanopoulos and Paraskevopoulos could do little and collapsed. Papandreou insisted that new elections would provide the country with solution to the crisis. He, fearing military intervention, took an historical step, even though he knew that members of his own party including his son Andreas would disapprove, when he decided to cooperate with the King and Panayiotis Kanellopoulos, who had succeeded Karamanlis as the leader of ERE, to prepare the country for elections (Gregoriades, 1975, Vol. 5, p. 40). Kanellopoulos, also suspecting military intervention, offered to head a new government and prepare the country for new elections. King Constantine appointed Kanellopoulos as Prime Minister on April 3, 1967. On April 15, the new Prime Minister dissolved parliament and elections were scheduled for May 27, 1967. The *ASPIDA* affair and the question of immunity for Andreas Papandreou as Member of Parliament dominated the campaign. The elections were not held because on April 21, 1967, at 1:30am, a group of junior officers launched a coup in an attempt to apply an old plan called *Prometheus*. The coup came at a time when "the younger leaders of Greek democracy were beginning to devise coherent reform plans" (Wilkinson & Hughes, 1998, p. 557). The coup ended the political crisis and ushered a new period of political strife.

Chapter 4

Military Dictatorship (1967-1974)

Greece was the first Western European country to experience a military dictatorship since the 1930s. In the morning of April 21st 1967, the residents of Athens woke up with tanks and military vehicles everywhere, and radio stations broadcasting military marching music. At 6:30am an anonymous message was communicated stating that because of the abnormal circumstances the military had decided to govern the country (Linardatos, 1986, p. 437). Most people inside and outside Greece were surprised. At first, there was concern about the political prisoners, but as time progressed the opinions of outsiders became polarized. Some thought that the dictators had "raped" Greek democracy; while others believed that the Greeks were incapable of living in a democratic system and were responsible for their fate (Zacharopoulos, 1976, p. 56). The inability of the power brokers on the Left, the Center and the Right to understand the Greek reality, and their inability to halt the movement toward military intervention created a climate of mistrust. Party officers, political activists and most youth did not trust the old political leaders and political parties (Yiannopoulos, 1976, pp. 258-259).

Although there were fears of a coup, there was almost no resistance from the Left or the Right. Even those in the highest ranks of the armed forces were startled. The question often asked is related to the reasons for the passivity of the higher echelon officers. It is believed that many thought of the coup as a movement directed from above, that is, under the auspices of the monarchy. In addition, a large percentage of the officers were much affected by the political atmosphere of the period and as a consequence were willing to tolerate the act of April 21, and for some time, the dictatorship itself (Gregoriades, 1975, Vol. 6, p. 36).

In spite of the pleas of Prime Minister Kanellopoulos, the King recognized the civilian government that served as a front for the troika of Georgios Papadopoulos, Nikolaos Makarezos and Stylianos Pattakos who had organized the coup and who were also referred to as the "Invisible Officers." The role of the King during the coup was not clear. The coup's leaders announced on April 21 that they had taken control of Greece with the monarchy's blessings. They also claimed that a royal decree had suspended Articles 5, 6, 8, 11, 12, 14, 18, 20, 95 and 97 of the constitution. The decree was fake because it was not signed by the King and he did not know anything about it (Gregoriades, 1975, Vol. 5, pp. 94-95). Others insisted that although the King first resisted the takeover, he later approved it by attending the ceremony when the new ministers were sworn in. It is argued that the King attended the ceremony because he wanted conservative politicians, like Constantine Kollias, to be included in the cabinet (Schwab & Frangos, 1970, p. 21). King Constantine himself said that he had been opposed to the coup, but accepted a temporary compromise believing that the country would soon return to parliamentary democracy (Gregoriades, 1975, Vol. 5, p. 100).

Constantine Kollias, Chief Prosecutor at the Supreme Court, was appointed, to his surprise, as the Prime Minister (Woodhouse, 1985, pp. 26-27). "A narrow, xenophobic, anti-intellectual tyranny descended on the country" (Wilkinson & Hughes, 1998, p. 557). On April 21, 1967, it was announced that the country was in a "state of siege under terms of a law passed in 1912. . . . The state-of-siege rules stipulated that: 1. Individuals can be apprehended and arrested without charge. They can be detained for any length of time. 2. There is no bail for political crimes. 3. All citizens, independent of position, can be brought before an emergency court-martial. 4. All gatherings, indoors and outdoors, are forbidden. All gatherings will be dissolved by force. 5. It is forbidden to form a syndicate (union) or group with labor union aims. Strikes are completely forbidden. 6. It is permitted to search houses, political premises, public buildings, all buildings, day and night, without special warrant. 7. It is forbidden to announce or publish any kind of information in any way through the press, radio and television without censorship beforehand. 8. Letters, telegrams and all means of communication will be censored. 9. Crimes, political crimes as well as those of the press, whether they have to do with private life or not, as well as the crimes to be judged by the court of appeal, will be judged by court-martial. 10. Everyone who commits a crime which should be punished by law, even if it is not against the army, will also be judged by court-martial" (Schwab & Frangos, 1970, p. 14).

Reasons for the Coup

Like Metaxas about thirty years earlier, the dictators adopted a populist rhetoric that clearly contradicted their economic and social policies (Clogg, 1987, p. 55). Constantine Kollias in a message to the people of Greece "spoke of the corruption of the political system, using for the first time the word *phavlokratia* (corruptocracy) which became the standard term of abuse under the dictatorship. He contrasted it with the new spirit of brotherhood, and emphasized the plebeian origins of the country's saviors: we belong to the working class. He defined the government's purpose merely as to restore the health of public life—a phrase which had often been used by Karamanlis ten years earlier" (Woodhouse, 1985, p. 30). He also said that there were not any more conservatives, centrists or leftists in Greece, there were only Greeks believing in Greece. Finally, he stated that under the appropriate circumstances Greece would quickly return to parliamentary democracy (Gregoriades, 1975, Vol. 5, p. 109). In the dictators' version of utopia, social classes would be abolished and a consensus on important issues would be achieved through systematic training (Veremis, 1997, p. 159). The leaders of the military regime constantly repeated their belief that the completion of their goals would result in the establishment of a "new parliamentary democracy," which would have constituted the desires of all the Greeks. But upon what principles was the "new democracy" to be based on? According to the dictators, the regime was governed by six principles. The principles were: no foreign interference in the affairs of Greece; the peaceful, and at the same time revolutionary, mission of the regime of April 21st; the democratic organization of the country's life; the determination of chronological limitations based on the circumstances; the completion of the goals of the *revolution;* and the priority of the public good (Pryroukis, 1983, pp. 18-20).

Based on these principles, the leaders of the military regime attempted, as they said, to realize the goals of the *revolution*. The goals, according to the protagonists and their supporters, were: to neutralize communism; to prevent the destruction of the economy; to politically, socially and economically reorganize Greece; to raise the living standards of the people; and to preserve the revolutionary character of the regime. These goals, according to the bearers, were guided by the revolutionary spirit of the military's intervention, and the military intervention took place in order to liberate the state from the cancerous past; to create a contemporary political conscience; to correctly implement the necessary social and economic measures that are required by an evolving reality; and to make it possible for the nation to move forward (Psyroukis, 1983, pp. 20-23).

Prior to the coup, the behavior of politicians and the prevailing political instability led many Greeks to develop an antipathy toward politics and politicians. The dictators reflected the same feelings and were determined to impose the military model of professionalism upon the government and the rest of the country. The military dictators first attempted to justify the coup by declaring that they were protecting the country from a communist takeover. While Papadopoulos stated that the communists had betrayed the nation and that the revolution was an historical necessity (Woodhouse, 1976, p. 3), Pattakos claimed that the government was preparing to provide Greek and international public opinion with 70 cars full of evidence of a communist conspiracy (Zormpalas, 1978, p. 13). Both assertions, of course, were incorrect. In fact, the unpreparedness of the left, something that was true of the other political parties too, led to the split of the Communist party in 1968 into two groups. One group remained loyal to the Soviet Union (the Communist Party of Greece of the Exterior) and the other (the Communist Party of Greece of the Interior) was Eurocommunist on outlook.

The members of the troika thought that they were defending the Helleno-Christian civilization from secular and western influences resulting from rapid social and economic changes. The dictators frequently used such terminology as *Epanastase*, which derives from the term *Anastase* or Resurrection/the Resurrection of Christ; *Hellas Aneste*, Greece has been resurrected; Hellas *Hellenon Christianon*, or Greece of Christian Greeks (Woodhouse, 1976, pp. 33-34). The dictators viewed themselves "as divinely chosen saviors of the nation" (Woodhouse, 1985, p. 20). They believed that Orthodoxy was inseparable from the nation, and Christianity was the continuation and culmination of the Greek spirit (Psyroukis, 1983, p. 20). The emphasis on Helleno-Christian values, of course, was an attempt to disguise martial law, torture, censorship, corruption, and nepotism.

The dictators thought that they were rescuing Greece from chaos resulting from the conflict between the monarchy and parliament. A conflict, which was enhanced during the years George Papandreou was in power. It was announced that one of the significant reasons for the *Revolution of April 21, 1967* was "to prevent division and the ready to explode civil conflict, which will lead to bloodshed and social and national ruin" (Digaves, 1975, p. 15). The dispute between the Prime Minister and King Constantine over control of the armed forces propelled the dictators to contend that democracy had collapsed by 1965. A curious contention because from 1967 to 1974 governments were either modified or completed six times.

There are those who believe that the coup d' etat resulted from the collision between the "status quo" and the "progressive forces." The first bloc was composed of the United States, the capitalists, the military, the monarchy, and ERE. The second group consisted of the lower and middle classes that found expression in the Center Union Party. Others believe that the coup resulted from the attempt of the middle class to gain its independence from United States hegemony. Furthermore, there are others who think that the *revolution* was a consequence of the conflict between the group that was pro-American and the group that was pro-European in orientation (Sakellaropoulos, 1998, pp. 33-55).

The Colonels, as the members of the troika became known, were from lower middle-class background and resented the privileged political elite in Athens (Clogg, 1992, p. 163). An important, albeit less emphasized, cause of the coup was the professional grievances of a number of especially middle rank officers. During the Civil War, the Greek army had to expand quickly. After the Civil War, with the top posts limited, there were serious constraints regarding the possibilities for advancement. This led to dissatisfaction and frustration. Able officers were often prevented from advancing and less qualified ones were preserved (Veremis, 1983, p. 179). However, the most important reason for the coup was directly connected to the threat that the greater political mobilization that had occurred in Greece presented to the dominance of the military and to its corporate interests. Important army officers feared substantial budget cuts for the armed forces and loss of institutional autonomy (Danopoulos & Gerston, 1990, p. 532; Mouzelis, 1987, p. 251). To the Colonels, the possible return of George Papandreou to power was not desirable. They believed that a Center Union victory would have meant a revision of the King's constitutional powers to prevent his resisting the retirement of numerous officers, the destruction of the royalist and anti-communist quality of the officer corps and the end of many personal careers (Campbell & Sherrard, 1968, p. 283).

In spite of the claims, the junta was unquestionably reactionary and suspicious of almost everything (Wilkinson & Hughes, 1998, p. 557). Members of the junta "called themselves collectively *the Revolution* (Woodhouse, 1985, p. 31), *or the Revolution of April 21 1967*. Georgios Papadopoulos stated that *the Revolution* was necessary to save what were at risk, to rescue the nation, and to offer to it the essentials and fundamentals that it did not posses. Furthermore, Papadopoulos said that the people of Greece had decided to rebel in order to secure their democratic liberties, to cut-off the ties to the past and to realize their dreams (Psyroukis, 1983, p. 16). The act of April 21, 1967, of course, was not a revolution. As Woodhouse (1985) states, it was not a revolution because a revolution "has a legal connotation in Greece, where there have been many revolutions. A revolution, once it has prevailed, is deemed to become legitimate and to create its own law. A coup d' etat is an illegal act, whose decrees are invalid. By a vote of the restored Parliament in 1975, it was declared that the Colonels had perpetrated not a revolution but a coup d' etat" (p. 12).

Ideology of the Junta

The leaders of the junta did not have a well thought-out ideology. Their "ideology" consisted of vaguely related statements. Pattakos proclaimed that the purpose of *the Revolution* was "to fashion a New Man" and this changed person "must have the strength to do Absolute Good" (Woodhouse, 1985, p. 31). He also said that the armed forces were the guardians of the sacred love for the country, of the belief in Christ, of the devotion to the family, and of the love and sacrifice taught by Christ on the Cross. Prime Minister Kollias stated that those in power did not belong to any political party, or the economic oligarchy. Instead, they stood by the side of the working class. Their basic purpose, he said, was social justice (Clogg, 1976, pp. 82-83). Papadopoulos came near to stating an ideology in a speech at Thessaloniki on August 28, 1971, when he attempted to define democracy. He said, "Responsible democracy . . . cannot be merely that democracy which is expressed by the casting and canvassing of votes. . . . There is no possibility of democracy as practiced in the past ever returning to Greece. . . . Democracy means the exercise of responsible authority on the part of the representatives of the people for the satisfaction of the public interest" (Woodhouse, 1985, p. 32). The junta, nonetheless, was fiercely anticommunist and nationalist.

The Colonels were against the whole ideological spectrum and political dissidents were imprisoned, exiled, or under house arrest. From the beginning the base of the dictatorship was the army. Officers who were not forced to retire gained both socially and financially from the 1967 coup. They therefore did not have an incentive to return power to civilian authorities. The navy and air force did not participate in the 1967 coup and played no significant role in the dictators' government, and naval officers were involved in the 1973 unsuccessful coup (Veremis, 1997, p. 161). On April 27, 1967, Papadopoulos stated that "we have here a sick man, whom we have on the operating table, and if the surgeon does not strap him down for the duration of the operation on the operating table, there is a possibility instead of the operation giving him the restoration of his health, it may lead to his death" (Woodhouse, 1985, p. 33). He continued by saying that the restrictions imposed were necessary for the sick man to undergo the surgery without any danger. When asked how long the recovery would last, he asserted that everything depended upon the seriousness of the illness (Gregoriades, 1975, Vol. 5, p. 123).

According to Papadopoulos, the task of the *Revolution* was to make a return to the past impossible. This was to be accomplished not only by reforming various institutions, but more important by reforming the individual Greeks. He proclaimed: "We must change our habits of thought and rid ourselves of individualism." . . . "Individuals must cease to be anarchic, materialistic individuals, and must become social individuals." . . . "We are now at the stage of trying to combine the two systems of rule by the individual with their harmonic division, where individual interest and individual initiative, while not being limited in an oppressive manner by the influences and by the interests of collectivity, are none the less made to move always within a predetermined framework" (Athenian, 1972, p. 115).

On April 27 a decree was issued abolishing all political parties. Ilias Iliou, the leader of EDA, was harshly treated and at least one member of the Communist party was killed. George Papandreou was held in a military hospital, his son Andreas was in the Averoff prison, and Kanellopoulos was under house arrest. Civil servants, especially in government offices, education and the judicial system, were purged. Labor unions were dissolved and their assets confiscated. Foreign governments became critical of the military regime and, on the domestic front; politicians did not want to associate themselves with the Colonels. The exception was Panayiotis Pipinelis, he had briefly succeeded Karamanlis as Prime Minister in 1963. Pipinelis on November 20, 1967, was appointed Foreign Minister believing the promises of the dictators of a return to parliamentary democracy.

King Constantine's actions made the situation even worse for the junta. The monarchy was a problem for the dictators from the beginning. Although some wanted to eliminate the monarchy, others were not in a hurry to abolish it. The monarchy was useful to them as long as the King acted as their mouthpiece, he had support in the armed forces and especially the navy, and he had popular support in some provincial areas (Woodhouse, 1985, pp. 33-35). In 1967 King Constantine was presented with a list of about 150 officers earmarked for early retirement. Since most of the officers on the list were friends of the Crown, King Constantine was confronted with a dilemma of either going against the junta or losing his remaining influence within the army (Veremis, 1997, pp. 161-162). Nearly seven months after the humiliation and loss of power King Constantine had suffered on April 21, he finally launched a counter-coup on December 13, 1967, in northern Greece with the involvement of Prime Minister Kollias. The King said that he had to accept the 1967 coup in order to avoid bloodshed, but he was no longer willing to allow the consolidation of the junta's power. He also called upon the people of Greece to assist him in reestablishing the moral values, which were born in Greece and from which civilized people continue to derive inspiration (Schwab & Frangos, 1970, pp. 43-45). The counter-coup failed and on December 14, the King went into exile. He flew to Rome with his family and some close supporters including Prime Minister Kollias and George Plytas, Mayor of Athens. The counter-coup failed because: a. Most of the military knew of the impending attempt; b. there was little coordination among the officers involved; c. of the decision not to use weapons, despite the military nature of the act; d. of the haste that the day of the coup was decided; e. of the lack of will among leading members of the counter-coup to fight; f. of the innate contradictions among members of the military; g. of a badly conceived and executed plan (Gregoriades, 1975, Vol. 5, pp. 218-219); and h. despite the professional competence of the king's loyal officers, they "were no much for the Colonels in conspiratorial skills" (Veremis, 1997. p. 162). After the King fled to Italy, the military was purged of all royalist elements and from 1967 to 1968 one sixth of the officers were either dismissed or retired (Veremis, 1997, p. 162).

On the 14th of December, Archbishop Ieronymos administered the oath of office as Regent to General Zoitakis. Stylianos Pattakos said that the "King was deemed to have deserted his duties, but not to have abdicated or been deposed" (Woodhouse, 1985, p. 48). The monarchy was placed under the custody of the military and General Zoitakis appointed Papadopoulos in place of Kollias as Prime Minister. Papadopoulos also became the Minister of Defense and the junta seemed to have emerged stronger than before. Papadopoulos was portrayed as a powerful opponent of the nation's enemies and as a person who was determined to convert Greece into a modern disciplined democratic country.

The junta now had a monopoly of power. Yet the dictators were still faced with a serious problem. King Constantine, although defeated, was not annihilated. To many foreign governments, he represented legitimacy and Papadopoulos was afraid that the King would establish a government-in-exile, which would have attracted foreign support. To prevent that from happening, the leader of the junta proposed the idea of the King's return under certain conditions. The King refused and in 1968, a fraudulent plebiscite was held to ratify a new constitution. According to final referendum figures, 91.87 percent of the people voted in support of the constitution. "Beneath this constitutional façade, the rulers sought a permanent and pervasive role for the armed forces" (Danopoulos & Gerston, 1990, p. 534).

Although an attempt was made, in August 1968, by Alexandros Panaghoulis to assassinate Papadopoulos, the opposition was scattered and unorganized. Panaghoulis, of course, did not succeed and was sentenced to death. Foreign protest convinced Papadopoulos to change the punishment to imprisonment. Mass opposition was limited because the "secret" police (ESA) harshly treated those who opposed the junta. Also, mass opposition was not widespread because "given the overwhelming power of the State and the fact that the working-class movement had been catastrophically defeated and physically decimated in the Civil war, armed resistance could find no popular base; . . . the working class was not prepared either for organized civil opposition to the junta's seizure of power" (Mouzelis, 1978, p. 129). Furthermore, the contained opposition resulted from the fact that the dictators were able to maintain, at least until 1973, satisfactory economic growth. The ineptness of the Colonels could not reverse the momentum of economic expansion that began in the 1950s. The leaders of the junta argued that by 1967, Greece was in economic ruin and they had succeeded in stabilizing the currency and promoting economic progress. The first part of their assertion was incorrect because the economic prosperity had begun during the decade of 1950, which was a consequence of the development plans put in place especially from 1957 to 1966. On the other hand, the claim of the Colonels that they had successfully managed the economy was true, and in particular in the large urban centers where the rising standard of living had not been interrupted (Pesmazoglou, 1976, p. 136). From 1960 to 1967, the GNP grew at an annual average rate of 6.7 percent. Under the dictatorship the GNP grew as follows:

		Percent
1967	-	4.5
1968	-	5.8
1969	-	8.8
1970	-	7.5
1971	-	7.3
1972	-	10.5
1973	-	10.1

Source: Data from N. Poulantzas (1976). *The Crisis of the Dictatorships: Portugal, Greece, Spain* (17). London: Humanities Press.

Failure to Achieve Legitimacy

Why did the military regime, despite the very low level of resistance, fail to achieve legitimacy and to consolidate itself? According to Nancy Bermeo (1995), the real barriers to the legitimation of the junta were institutional and cultural rather than economic (p. 450). The nature of both the party system and the military explain some of the developments. Democracy had served the interests primarily of the Conservative Right and the high-ranking military officers. In 1967, although important changes in the electorate had taken place, the conservative party (ERE) continued to be a dominant force. ERE controlled the Greek political system since the end of the Civil War, with the exception of 1963-1965 when the Center Union of George Papandreou came to power. Panayiotis Kanellopoulos was willing to risk another election thinking that even if Papandreou were successful in the 1967 election, he would win the next (Bermeo, 1995, p. 450). The leader of ERE also said that even with a Center Union victory, he and Papandreou had agreed to collaborate in order to maintain tranquility (Gregoriades, 1975, Vol. 6, pp. 10-13) by forming a Center-Right coalition government. Both leaders acted as they did for the purpose of preventing a military takeover (Katres, 1974, p. 80).

While the willingness of some conservative leaders to have elections was based on the belief that the electoral results could be manipulated, others wanted to go ahead with elections because of certain qualities of the Greek political culture. Greece introduced universal male suffrage in 1864, before Great Britain, and the nineteenth century constitutions were the most democratic in Europe. Even though these constitutions were never fully implemented, the fact that they were written and passed suggests that there was an interest in democracy among members of the Greek elite during the early days of the Greek modern state (Bermeo, 1995, pp. 450-451). It is true that Greek democracy prior to 1974 was flawed and exclusionary, but it is also true that the longevity of the Greek parliamentary system since the mid-nineteenth century could be rivaled by few European states (Veremis, 1987, p. 214).

The breakup of the coalition among the conservative Right, the monarchy, and the army resulted from the military's attempt to by itself gain full control of the Greek political system. Cut off from power, the King and the Right reacted by not supporting the military dictatorship. Because the monarch gradually decided to oppose the dictatorship, a large number of the political elite also refused to support the regime. The Crown's opposition also led to divisions within the armed forces: while many navy and air force officers opposed the junta, many in the army supported the regime. As the opposition of the monarchy contributed to the lack of legitimacy of the dictatorship, the non-cooperation of the Right also inhibited its consolidation. Three factors made this outcome possible: first, the attempts by the junta to resurrect the anticommunist state had become unacceptable to the majority of the Greeks; second, the rejection by the junta of Greek parliamentary institutions as corrupt and easily penetrated by communists; and third, the junta's attacks against the political elites which were denounced as inept and corrupt, and responsible for the moral degeneration of the Greeks (Diamantouros, 1991, pp. 146-147).

The Greek military as an institution also explains the failure of the dictatorship to legitimize and consolidate itself. The military has had an history of internal purges and has always been characterized by divisions between the high ranking members (members of the bourgeoisie) and low ranking offices (of peasant background), who launched the coup; between the various branches of the armed forces; and between "democrats" and "authoritarians" (Bermeo, 1995, p. 451). In addition, the junta isolated itself from officers who believed that the military would be damaged by associating themselves with a group of conspirators who were enriching themselves. The naval mutiny of 1973 was an indication of the growing alienation. Finally, serious disagreements among core members of the junta regarding the path it should take resulted in the overthrow of Papadopoulos by Ioannidis in November 1973 (Verney & Couloumbis, 1991, pp. 108-109).

The climate in Europe, as well as elsewhere, also decreased the likelihood of consolidation and legitimation of the junta. Democratic principles, unlike authoritarian ones, are widely accepted, and an increasing number of regional and international organizations are committed to the promotion of democracy and being democratic is a condition that must be satisfied for membership (Diamantouros, 1991, p. 146). An example is the European Union, the members of which are democratic and a country is not permitted to join unless its economic and democratic political system is stable. When Greece became a member of the European Community (now the European Union) in 1981, it was made clear that the relationship will continue as long as Greece remained democratic. Given the financial dependence on the European Community/European Union, an overthrow of the civilian democratic government would prove costly (Verney & Couloumbis, 1991, pp. 118-119). "In other words, a powerful external guarantee of both democratic consolidation and balanced growth would result" (Dunphy, 1995, p. 143).

In spite of the lack of legitimacy, and regardless of the fact that the military regime was brutal and publicly condemned by its European allies, nothing concrete was done against it. More importantly, the United States, seen by many Greeks as responsible for the coup, followed a "curious" policy toward the junta. The United States government viewed the dictatorship as a bastion of anticommunism and of stability in the western Mediterranean. The government of the United States considered three options in dealing with the junta: first, to support it; second, to break off relations with it; and third, to maintain relations with it while pushing for return to constitutional government. It chose the latter because of Greece's membership in NATO and the expanded activities of the Soviet fleet in the Mediterranean (Woodhouse, 1985, p. 87). The United States Undersecretary of State, Roger Davis, clearly stated his government's position when he said that: "We do not agree with the present political system in Greece and we believe that return to democracy is essential precondition for the long-term stability and prosperity of Greece. Simultaneously, we are obliged to protect our considerable strategic interests in Greece, which is an important location in the critical region of the eastern Mediterranean" (Couloumbis, 1978, p. 40). During the years of the dictatorship, the United States endeavored to balance these two conflicting interests, and as a consequence, the dictators remained in power for seven years. Of course, there are those who disagree and believe that the junta was just an instrument of the United States. As Couloumbis (1975) says: "the military dictatorship that was proclaimed-without much domestic support and with very limited international legitimacy-was completely dependent, for its survival, on outside agents and specifically the United States" (pp. 18-19).

Disintegration of the Dictatorship

The disintegration of the military dictatorship commenced when important political elites decided to withdraw their support and could no longer accept stability at any price. By mid-1972, members of the business community, including Stavros Niarchos and Aristotle Onassis, began to have reservations regarding the regime's stability (Danopoulos & Gerston, 1990, p. 536). Furthermore, serious economic problems emerged in the 1970s. In discussing Greece, Portugal and Spain, Vergopoulos (1990) says that "the great upheaval of the world system should not be imputed to the oil or energy markets but much rather to the international financial circuits based on an autonomous dynamism beyond any control by the nation states. This new international financial reality, with its corollary, the generalization, on a world scale, of restrictive policies aimed at controlling prices and bolstering national currencies, brutally reversed the flow of financial resources away from the countries of Southern Europe. The rapid spread of financial difficulties within the three countries, traditionally dependent upon the inflow of foreign currencies . . . was at the origin of the new policies in the south of Europe aimed at providing equilibrium and financial control at the price of a slow down or even a halt in growth" (p. 145).

A significant factor that contributed to the demise of the junta was the lack of cohesiveness within the military. There were three distinct groups, each one having its own vision regarding the *Revolution of 1967*. The first group desired a return to the barracks so that the military be able to fulfill its mission and protect the country. The second group, led by Papadopoulos, advocated a degree of "democratization." The third group, the hard liners and also known as *Kadofides*, wanted to perpetuate military rule (Danopoulos & Gerston, 1990, pp. 536-537).

Additionally, college students occupied the Law Faculty at the University of Athens and in May 1973 naval officers plotted to overthrow the regime. The mutiny on the destroyer *Velos* demonstrated to the rest of Europe that the dictators did not have complete control of all the officers (Veremis, 1997, pp. 164-165). Since the King had commanded the loyalty of navy officers, George Papadopoulos blamed the King for instigating the coup from his exile in Rome. Papadopoulos replaced the monarchy with a presidential republic. The government announced that the 1968 constitution would be amended and Papadopoulos was proclaimed as provisional President until a plebiscite was held scheduled for July 29, 1973. The plebiscite was held and was characterized by ballot manipulation and voter fraud. The government announced that it received 78.4 percent of the vote and Papadopoulos was confirmed as President for eight years. Papadopoulos granted amnesty, freed political prisoners, relaxed censorship and proceeded to appoint Spyros Markezinis "to oversee elections, the proposed first stage in the introduction of a 'guided' democracy" (Clogg, 1992, p. 167). The elections were scheduled for February 1974.

Since the plebiscite was conducted under repressive conditions and ballot manipulation, the political opponents of the regime became reenergized. Unlike the 1968 plebiscite, this one provoked great criticism. Politicians, inside and outside prison, met and began to regroup after years of "muffled opposition." Their hatred of the junta enabled them to put aside differences and to prepare the ground for "a post-regime process of civilian renewal" (Veremis, 1997, p. 165). The government of Markezinis lasted from October 8 to November 25, 1973. The *Markezinis experiment* was acceptable to a small group of conservative politicians who viewed his government as an important bridge on the road toward parliamentary democracy. A second group of politicians, headed by Karamanlis, wanted to keep its distance and sought guarantees that the elections would be honest. A third group, led by Kanellopoulos, Mavros and Papandreou, refused to participate in the elections and to recognize Markezinis' government. Finally, a fourth group headed by Iliou supported participation in the elections as a means to weaken the junta (Anastasiades, 1993, p. 10).

The rule of Papadopoulos as President was short-lived. By 1973, the divisions within the junta became more apparent. The hard-liners wanted to stay in power just because they wanted to do so and they also opposed the "democratization" attempts undertaken by Papadopoulos. Unlike the hard-liners, Papadopoulos realized that the purpose of *the Revolution* was to do something new. He did not exactly know what needed to be done and he failed to recognize the magnitude of the threats to his position. He had opponents in the navy and the army, and he never took seriously the threat posed by the university students.

Before the elections, large-scale demonstrations began in Athens and university students occupied the Polytechnic School on November 15, 1973. The next day the police failed to disperse the students. On November 17, the junta brutally suppressed the students: 23 people were killed and over 1,000 were injured or badly mistreated (Gregoriades, 1975, Vol. 7, p. 145). Papadopoulos and his government were overthrown by military hard-liners led by Brigadier Dimitrios Ioannidis who was the head of the military police and who believed that Papadopoulos "had adulterated the principles of 21 April 1967" (Veremis, 1997, p. 167). Ioannidis believed that he was preventing the *Revolution* from digressing into corruption. Lieutenant-General Phaidon Ghizikis was chosen as President. The events surprised everyone and no authority, including the government and the police, expected the events that had just transpired.

The developments of November 1973 coincided with the deterioration of relations with Turkey caused primarily by the discovery of oil near the northern Aegean island of Thasos. The Turkish government claimed the right to explore for oil in the Aegean. "Against the background of the dispute in the Aegean, the Ioannidis regime adopted an increasingly menacing line towards Cyprus, seeking to force a reluctant President Makarios to accept Athens as the 'national center' of Hellenism" (Clogg, 1992, p. 168) and to force Makarios to accept union with Greece. In early July 1974, President Makarios demanded the removal of the mainland Greek officers in the Cyprus National Guard. Ioannidis, desiring to improve his standing among the Greeks, initiated a Sampson-led coup against the President who was forced to flee the island. Five days later, the Turkish government, fearing that the coup was a prelude to *enosis* or union with Greece and for the purpose of reestablishing "constitutional order" on the island, decided to invade the northern part of Cyprus on July 20, 1974, "which finally drove the nail into the coffin of the Colonels' dictatorship" (Verney & Couloumbis, 1991, pp. 111-112).

Greece and Turkey mobilized their forces and the possibility of war between them was clear. Ioannidis ordered the air force and the navy to attack Turkish positions in Cyprus, and he ordered the army to prepare for operations against Turkey in Thrace. Following his orders would have meant military disaster. Lacking support inside and outside Greece, the Ioannidis regime collapsed. "The senior military officers of the three services decided that a return to civilian rule was opportune and forced the ouster of Ioannidis. Faced with a mutiny of his top military commanders, Ioannidis reluctantly acceded to their demands that he not oppose their decision to call back the former civilian leaders" (Psomiades, 1982, p. 252).

Phaidon Ghizikis called for an emergency meeting of some of the most important politicians and senior army officers. The transfer of power from the military to the civilian leadership took place in two stages on July 23 and 24. In the first stage, a group of military and old political leaders-the President of the Republic, and the chiefs of the armed forces, the army, the navy and the air force; George Athanassiades-Novas, Petros Garoufalias and Stefanos Stefanopoulos who had played a significant role in 1965 when the Center Union party lost its majority in parliament and which precipitated the constitutional crisis that led to the 1967 coup; Markezinis who was chosen by the junta to begin the "democratization" experiment that ended in November 1973; Panayiotis Kanellopoulos and Evangelos Averoff-Tossizza, prominent members of the conservative Right; Xenophon Zolotas, a respected conservative banker; and George Mavros, a member of the Center Union prior to 1967 (Diamantouros, 1991, p. 157) met to consider the format under which power would be transferred. The civilian leadership rejected Phaidon Ghizikis' proposal to retain those holding the ministries of Defense, Public Order and Interior. The civilian leadership also rejected Markezinis' suggestion for a non-political government under the conservative diplomat Christianos Xanthopoulos-Palamas (Diamantouros, 1984, p. 54).

In the second stage, the military and the civilian leaders invited Constantine Karamanlis to return from his exile in France to "oversee the dismemberment of the dictatorship and the return to democratic government" (Clogg, 1992, p. 168). Karamanlis accepted the offer under two conditions: first, the armed forced would not interfere in the political life of Greece, and second, all the political forces would support his efforts (Anastasiades, 1993, pp. 15-16; Katrakis, 1993, p. 15). On July 24, 1974, at 4 am he was sworn in as Prime Minister of Greece. During these difficult times, Karamanlis became a national symbol (Tourkovasilis-Galanos, 1980, p. 81). The Karamanlis solution was accepted after a last minute proposal to transfer power to the leaders of the two major parties, Panayiotis Kanellopoulos, the head of ERE as Prime Minister, and George Mavros, the head of the Center Union as deputy Prime Minister, was rejected (Diamantouros, 1984, p. 55). The important actors in Greek politics decided to revive a "previously employed constitutional format" (Schmitter, 1996, p. 83) and "freedom was restored to Greece as though by magic" (Wilkinson & Hughes, 1998, p. 558). As Maxwell and Spiegel (1994) say, "the dramatic social and economic changes that occurred during the later years of the Franco regime were important to the establishment of a democratic regime" in Spain (p. 4). To an extent that also holds true in the case of Greece. Many forces conspired to undermine the military regime, and to facilitate the transition toward and the consolidation of democracy.

Chapter 5

Transition Toward Democracy

In a televised speech on July 25, 1974, Karamanlis declared that during "the life of all nations there are moments which impose moral and national exaltation. It is during these moments that a people, disappointed by the recent and distant past, seek with agony their way. It is these moments that our country is experiencing today" (Kartakis, 1993, p. 14). The transition[1] from dictatorship to democracy was realized in a climate of ambivalence. On the one hand, the advent of democratic politics was closely linked to national humiliation as a result of the inability of the junta to do much against Turkey after the invasion of Cyprus in the summer of 1974. On the other hand, because the dictators were in power only for seven years, the beginning of democratic politics signified not only a break from the authoritarian regime but also it demonstrated important continuities with the discredited pre-coup political system. This ambivalence contributed to the "emergence of a sincere yearning for a more radical break with the postwar period and for a 'truly new beginning'" (Diamantouros, 1991, p. 19). The collapse of the junta meant the end of the "institutional remnants" of the Civil War (Alivizatos, 1990, p. 133).

Karamanlis had to perform an exceptionally delicate balancing act in attempting to ensure a smooth transition from military dictatorship to pluralist democracy, and to avoid a war between Greece and Turkey. The Prime Minister concluded that war was not a realistic option based on the fact that the Greek military was in a ruinous state of disorder, that Cyprus is much closer to Turkey than to Greece, that the Turkish forces were already in Cyprus, and that Greece had received very little support from its allies. The United States was too preoccupied as a result of

President Nixon's resignation and the Secretary of State, Henry Kissinger, was slow to react because he considered Makarios as the *Castro* of the eastern Mediterranean. Great Britain, one of the guarantors of the 1960 constitution and whose colonial policies had created the Cyprus problem, did not want to do much to diffuse the crisis. The invasion of Cyprus resulted in the death of many, the displacement of approximately 200,000 people, the occupation by mainland Turkish troops of about 40 percent of the island, and anti-American demonstrations in Cyprus and Greece believing that United States foreign policy was supportive of Turkey. Instead of war, which according to Karamanlis would have weakened the defense of the country, the Prime Minister chose diplomacy (Kartakis, 1993, p. 19). Karamanlis withdrew Greece from the military wing of NATO and threatened to remove the American bases from Greece (Clogg, 1992, p. 170). A war was averted, but his protests did not bear much fruit because Turkish troops are still on the island. They occupy close to 30 percent of the country and Cyprus is still divided.

Karamanlis was the most suitable person to facilitate the transition from dictatorship to democracy. His program "of an orderly, sober democracy" (Wilkinson & Hughes, 1998, p. 558) was what most of the Greek citizens wanted. He was acceptable to the military, the anti-monarchist Right, and many in the center. Karamanlis was strongly anti-communist during most of the 1950s, he had dominated Greek politics until the early 1960s, and had gone into self-imposed exile in France following his clash with the King and defeat in the 1963 elections which first brought George Papandreou of the Center Union to power. Karamanlis' reputation remained untarnished because he was not directly involved in the events that led to the collapse of parliamentary politics in 1967. "The Karamanlis solution implied an unspoken decision to de-emphasize the role of existing political parties in the transition process and suggested instead a preference for leadership that stood 'above parties' and appealed to the 'nation' as a whole. This perspective, which Karamanlis shared with those who recalled him and which was in conformity with his charismatic image, was best reflected in the fact that he was initially invested with sole political power and only subsequently appointed the first members of his government" (Diamantouros, 1991, p. 159). Karamanlis helped reintegrate Greek society.

From July 24 and November 17, 1974, when national elections were held, Karamanlis' goals were: "to minimize commitments to collective and individual actors, to personalize crisis management, to maximize his freedom of movement and to create the preconditions for a genuine political democracy in Greece" (Diamantouros, 1991, p. 159). To accomplish these goals, Karamanlis adopted a course of action characterized by continuity, change, and gradualism. His government of national unity, sworn in on July 25 and 26, 1974, included established political figures from the Right and the Center. He did not include members of the Center-Left identified with Andreas Papandreou, nor members of the traditional Left, even though he included George Alexander Mangakis who was a socialist. Most of these individuals had anti-junta credentials. The make-up of his cabinet signified a shift from the uncompromising anti-Communist Right to the Center-Right (Diamantouros, 1991, pp. 159-160).

Karamanlis' gradualism became apparent with the incremental approach he followed in dealing with the most explosive popular demands including purges of the military, the bureaucracy, the universities, the security forces, and the prosecution of the architects of the 1967 coup. Karamanlis wanted to first hold national elections because he knew he would win, but also because he believed that until elections were held it could not be argued that the foundations of democracy had been laid. He deemed it necessary to legitimize his regime and then deal with the divisive issues. He had to take the necessary measures to ensure that important agencies and institutions (police, security services, intelligence agencies) were under civilian control. He also had to draw a line between retiring the officers who were strong supporters of the dictatorship and prosecuting them for offenses committed during the seven years they were in power (Diamantouros, 1991, pp. 160-161).

Asserting civilian control over the military was a difficult task. The armed forces were in disarray and the morale of the soldiers was low. Military presence in Athens was heavy making uncomfortable those who feared another take-over by the army. The first sign of the difficulties ahead was the dispute over the recall of naval officers dismissed during the period of the junta. The Chief of the armed forces, General Bonanos, opposed the move. But after a heated debate he was overruled. On August 11, 1974, when a war with Turkey was imminent, Prime Minister Karamanlis requested the removal of all tanks from Athens and their transfer to the north to protect Thrace. Once more Bonanos refused. Karamanlis informed Bonanos to follow his orders or he would ask the Minister of Public Order to relocate the tanks. Bonanos altered his position and the government's control of the military was established (Psomiades, 1982, pp. 256-257).

The election was held on November 17, 1974, and for the first time since World War II parties across the ideological spectrum were represented. The hastily organized parties remained "personal parties." Karamanlis founded New Democracy on September 28, 1974, PASOK's (created on September 3, 1974) organization and inspiration depended on its founder, Andreas Papandreou. Members of the Center Union chose George Mavros as their leader and the communists, although divided, succeeded in establishing the United Left coalition with Ilias Iliou at the helm. Newcomers entered the political arena, but, by and large, the old political class that had been pushed aside by the junta came back and retained control (Macridis, 1981, p. 10).

The November 17, 1974, election "was the first genuine free election in Greece since World War II; completely lacking was the pressure or intimidation usually engaged in by the forces of law and order" (Psomiades, 1982, p. 260). Karamanlis' New Democracy party (a version of the pre-1967 National Radical Union) won a massive victory, 54 percent of the popular vote and 219 out of 300 seats in parliament. The people of Greece voted for someone they could trust, for someone who was a known commodity and they were also much influenced by the slogan of *Karamanlis or the tanks*. "Implicit in New Democracy's electoral strategy was the projection of Karamanlis as the one person who would ensure the survival of democracy in Greece" (Psomiades, 1982, p. 260). New Democracy accentuated the personality of Karamanlis, and he underlined the need for change "without risks" (Macridis, 1981, p. 11). His opponents, on the other hand, did not offer any convincing alternatives.

One of the surprising outcomes of the 1974 election was the performance of the Center Union, which received 21 percent of the vote as compared to 53 percent of the vote it had received in the 1964 elections. A sign of things to come was the performance of the Panhellenic Socialist Movement (PASOK) headed by Andreas Papandreou. Although it was a new party, created within forty days after the collapse of the junta, without much organization and base, it won about 14 percent of the popular vote (Clogg, 1992, pp. 171-172). PASOK received much support in Athens and Thessaloniki as well as in less developed and conservative regions such as Macedonia and Epirus (Ioakimidis, 1984, p. 47). Obviously, the 1974 election was a triumph for Karamanlis. (See Table 5)

TABLE 5
Election of November 17, 1974

Political Party	No. of Votes	Percentage
New Democracy	2,631, 531	54.51
Center Union	984,584	20.40
PASOK	656,466	13.60
United Left	448,362	9.29
EDE (Extreme Right)	53,418	1.10
Independent	51,601	1.07

Source: Data from R.C. Macridis & T. Lancaster (1987). "The Politics of Greece." In R.C. Macridis (Ed.), *Modern Political Systems: Europe* (336). Englewood Cliffs, New Jersey: Prentice-Hall, Inc.

The parliamentary election of November 1974 was followed by a national referendum on the future of the monarchy. The King, who had been absent from Greece since the unsuccessful coup of 1967, had not returned to Greece after the fall of the dictatorship, and Karamanlis, still remembering the clashes with the monarchy in the 1960s, did not campaign on behalf the King and maintained ambiguous neutrality. The majority of the Greeks, 70 percent, voted in support of a republic and against the monarchy. The people of Greece welcomed the outcome with great enthusiasm.

Within just five months, Karamanlis not only legitimized his authority through honest elections but he also, through the referendum, resolved the debate over the institution of the monarchy. The monarchy had been imposed by the Protecting Powers as a price for independence during the nineteenth century, and had caused friction and political instability (Clogg, 1992, pp. 172-173). The voters electorally voided the almost 150-year tradition of monarchical rule. King Constantine did not dispute the results and said that national unity was paramount, wished that developments would justify the outcome of the referendum (Anastasiades, 1993, p. 39). Ten days after the referendum, the Members of Parliament chose Michael Stasinopoulos as temporary President. General Phaidon Ghizikis, who continued to be President after the fall of the junta, resigned. Amid strong opposition in parliament, caused by the considerable presidential powers, a new constitution was approved on June 7 and came into effect on June 11, 1975. According to the constitution a two-thirds majority in parliament is needed to elect the President for a five-year term. The President has the power to dissolve parliament and can initiate a referendum on any important issue concerning the country. The President also has the power to proclaim martial law and has final control of the armed forces (Smith, 1986, p. 291). The first President of the Republic, Konstantinos Tsatsos, was elected on June 19, 1975.

Karamanlis was now in a position to begin the *apohountopoiisi* or de-juntification of the system. Nonetheless, he had to proceed carefully because an indiscriminate revenge would have led to strong reaction from junta supporters. That was an obvious possibility as demonstrated by the unsuccessful February 1975 plot, the so-called Conspiracy of 39, against Karamanlis and Makarios who had returned to Cyprus in December 1974. During 1975 a number of televised trials were held of those responsible for the 1967 coup, of the leaders of the 1975 plot, of those responsible for the brutal suppression of the Polytechnic uprising, and those responsible for the torturing of prisoners from 1967 to 1974. The sentences handed down were harsh. Ioannidis received a seven-fold life sentence; the original troika of Papadopoulos, Makarezos and Pattakos were sentenced to death. Karamanlis well aware of how the execution of military leaders after the Asia Minor catastrophe had poisoned interwar Greek political life commuted the death sentences to life imprisonment. Despite criticism from the opposition for exercising excessive restraint, the new democratic government was successful in dealing with the "legacy problem" and the fact that those who were given life sentences are still in prison, with the exception of those who have died of course, served as a warning to those thinking to subvert the democratic institutions (Clogg, 1992, pp. 173-174).

Consolidation of Democracy

The transition toward democracy began with Karamanlis' arrival in Greece on July 21, 1974, and ended on December 9, 1974, when parliament opened and Karamanlis became accountable to parliament, the quickest in Southern Europe. However, what caused the transitional period to be so brief? The first reason was the nonhierarchical nature of the 1967 coup as evidenced by the purging, at the advent of the coup, of about 400 senior officers. Therefore, the base of support for the coup within the military was limited. The second reason was the intensification of the political mobilization of civil society by 1973, climaxed by the student occupation of the Polytechnic School. Because the Colonels' base of support was so limited, the students were the recipients of widespread popular support, which further divided the military. The third reason was the inability of the junta to respond to the Cyprus crisis on July 20, 1974, when Turkish troops invaded the northern part of the island. Upper echelon officers intervened and forced Ioannidis and the hard-liners to step down and transfer power to civilians. The fourth reason was the decision by high-ranking officers to transfer power to the civilians. Hence, they acted as part of the state and not the military regime. The fifth reason was the inability of the military as an institution to impose, because of the urgency to remove the armed forces from government, any conditions for the removal of officers. The sixth reason was the decision by the civilian government to reinstate the once removed high-ranking officers. The seventh reason was the fact that the transfer of power by a state institution (the high-ranking officers) to a caretaker democratic government prevented any kind of revolution (Linz, Stepan & Gunther, 1995, p. 111; Linz & Stepan, 1996, pp. 130-131).

In approximately five months after the collapse of the junta and the return of Karamanlis, the basic institutional arrangements establishing a true democracy in Greece had been completed. In the years that followed, the Left re-entered the political arena and the Center-Left (PASOK) came to power, which signified the end of about fifty years of almost uninterrupted control of Greek politics by the Right. Furthermore, Karamanlis was elected as President of Greece in 1980 and New Democracy chose a successor to Karamanlis. In spite of the weaknesses, the political system of Greece since 1974 has been the most open, inclusive and democratic in Modern Greek history (Diamantouros, 1991, p. 163). Greek democracy is characterized by broad-based suffrage, free and open elections, freedom of speech and assembly, the rule of law, government accountability to parliament, and an independent judiciary. In Greek democracy, there is also a "continuous interaction between formal institutions and ever-evolving popular participation (Andrews & Chapman, 1995, p. 5). This is a development of serious significance for modern Greece considering that "democracy as a concept and practice was vague and largely alien for most Greeks" (Hadjiyannis, 1990, p. 139).

The transition toward and consolidation of democracy took place during time of great tension between Greece and Turkey. The external threat gave Karamanlis the opportunity to promote his agenda without much opposition. As Winston Churchill said in his memoirs: "The Greeks are constantly fighting among themselves and the only time they cooperate is when confronted with an external threat" (Tourkovasilis-Galanos, 1980, p. 81). Diamantouros (1991) also states that: "There can be no doubt that, in the absence of these conditions, Karamanlis would have been quickly and strenuously opposed from a number of quarters: at the very least, the whole process would have been more protracted and the end-result quite different" (pp. 163-164). Even though the 1974 crisis resulting from the Turkish invasion of Cyprus was defused, tension remained high because of the fortification of the Aegean islands by Greece, the differences over the continental self in the Aegean, the continuous presence of mainland Turkish troops in Cyprus, and the disputes over air traffic control in the Aegean. But the serious economic and international problems did not upset the unprecedented political stability between 1974 and 1977, when new elections were held.

Prime Minister Karamanlis was preoccupied with foreign policy issues. He sought European Community membership before 1984, which was a possibility according to the 1961 treaty of association. Greece became a member of the European Community in January 1981. His government began to renegotiate Greece's position in NATO; to reconsider the future of the United States bases in Greece; to improve relations with the United States damaged during the years of the military dictatorship; and to improve relations with Balkan neighbors. The immense need to reform agriculture, education, social security and health care was sidelined because they were issues of domestic policy and as such of low priority. Yet democracy survived in Greece.

The election of November 20, 1977, was free, open and highly contested. Karamanlis and his New Democracy party stressed their accomplishments as related to the stabilization and democratization of the country, as well as the gradual enactment of reforms. New Democracy became even more committed to democratic principles because of the emergence of the National Front, an extreme right wing party. The National Front gained about 7 percent of the vote. Karamanlis disassociated himself from this extremist party and moved closer to the center. But "while in 1974 there had been a widespread perception that the only he stood between democracy and dictatorship, in 1977 there were no such constraints on voting behavior. New Democracy's share of the vote fell by 12 percentage points from 54 to 42" (Clogg, 1992, p. 178).

The most significant electoral changes occurred at the center and center-left. The Center Union virtually collapsed as a political party. Its share of the vote dropped from 20.4 percent in 1974 to 12 percent in 1977. The greatest beneficiary was PASOK under Andreas Papandreou. PASOK gained 25.3 percent of the popular vote, up from 13.5 percent in 1974 (Lancaster, 1990, p. 268). As seen in Table 6, although PASOK was a new political party, founded in 1974, it became the main opposition because of Papandreou's nationalist rhetoric, his criticism of the European Community and NATO, his uncompromising stand toward Turkey, and its nationwide organizational structure. PASOK "was shaped by recent Greek history and the particular conditions of the time. These were likely to make it introverted and hostile to West European integration" (Verney, 1996, p. 175). Papandreou brilliantly exploited the resentment felt by many Greeks toward the NATO allies and especially the United States (Clogg, 1993, p. ix). Also, PASOK, as a new party, had an advantage over the others because it was not connected to the difficult past. PASOK's success made many New Democracy leaders realize that they too needed to modernize and better organize their party.

TABLE 6
Election of November 20, 1977

Political Party	No. of Votes	Percentage
National Front (extreme right)	346,800	6.84
New Democracy	2,122,894	41.88
Democratic Center Union	607,985	12.00
PASOK	1,282,577	25.31
Coalition of the Left (Eurocommunist)	136,712	2.70
KKE (pro-Soviet)	470,852	9.29
Other	100,147	1.98

Source: Data from Roy C. Macridis and Thomas D. Lancaster (1987). "The Politics of Greece." In Roy C. Macridis (Ed.), *Modern Political Systems: Europe* (337). Englewood Cliffs, New Jersey: Prentice-Hall, Inc.

However, Karamanlis, who continued to be preoccupied with foreign policy, did not modernize and democratize New Democracy. All other issues compared to foreign policy and European Community matters were of secondary importance to him (Katsoudas, 1991, p. 4). The creation of New Democracy by Karamanlis was an attempt to modernize the traditional Right (ERE). But although the party introduced "new personnel into Greek politics (127 out of its 220 Mps ran for office for the first time in 1974), its leadership consisted exclusively of ex-ERE members. New Democracy failed essentially to project a convincing image of a modern, center-right party, and this was directly related to its inability to formulate and articulate a coherent ideology and to create a well-structured mass organization" (Lyrintzis, 1984, p. 106). Karamanlis' desire to be viewed as a national rather than a party leader caused him to neglect party ideology and organization (Katsoudas, 1991, p. 5). New Democracy also failed to modernize the Greek bureaucracy and to minimize clientilism.

In May 1980, when the first President's, Konstantinos Tsatsos, five-year term expired, Karamanlis was elected by parliament as the new President. The opposition parties welcomed the election of the new President with reservation. Karamanlis himself stated that he wished to cooperate with the party in power to solidify democracy and to strengthen national unity. Georgios Rallis, who did not posses the qualities of Karamanlis, became the leader of New Democracy, and on May 10, 1980, he was sworn in as Prime Minister. Factionalism and divisions prevailed within New Democracy under Rallis. And now that the presidency was in the secure hands of Karamanlis, the Greek voters believed that they could take the risk of voting for the unpredictable Papandreou during the elections of October 18, 1981. Papandreou himself realized that had to move toward the center in order to win elections. He recognized that the slogans of the 1970s were not as appropriate during the 1980s. Gone were the days when he wanted to pull Greece out of the European Community and NATO, as well as to close down the United States bases in Greece. Everything was up for negotiation (Clogg, 1992, p. 180). PASOK's initial hostility toward the West was a product of more than 150 years of foreign interference in Greek affairs. Papandreou and many of his contemporaries viewed foreign influence as a threat to Greek democracy (Verney, 1996, p. 173).

The election of Karamanlis as President aided Papandreou in two ways: First, it eliminated the prospect of a difficult battle between the two charismatic personalities. Second, it substituted a "charismatic duel" with a "charismatic tandem," a powerful and moderate President acting as a counterweight to a more radical Prime Minister (Mavrogordatos, 1983a, p. 20). Papandreou was interested in the social transformation of Greece and he made promises ranging from the objective teaching of history to eliminating the nefos or smog covering Athens. The slogan used was *Allaghi* or change, which appealed to many and especially the young voters. New Democracy, which ran on the platform of *Ananeossis* or renewal, was incapable of responding to the PASOK challenge and in the elections of 1981 Papandreou's party emerged as the victor. PASOK won 48.06 percent of the vote and 172 out of 300 seats in parliament. New Democracy's percentage of the vote dropped from 42 to 35.86 percent (Clogg, 1992, p. 182). New Democracy's poor performance forced the resignation of Georgios Rallis and the election of Evangelos Averoff-Tossizza as its new leader.

As seen in Table 7, the elections of October 18, 1981, caused the bipolarization of the already fragmented traditional party system and the almost total extinction of the centrist parties. The Greek Left (including the socialists) scored an impressive victory by gaining over 60 percent of the vote. This was a remarkable accomplishment considering the fact that the Left was regarded as 'legal' for only seven years (Demetras, 1991, p. 295).

TABLE 7
Election of October 18, 1981

Political Party	No. of Votes	Percentage
New Democracy	2,033,584	35.86
PASOK	2,725,132	48.06
Center	23,723	0.42
Communist	619,292	10.92
Communist (Eurocommunist)	77,461	1.37
Liberals and Assorted Centrists	165,653	3.30
Extreme Left	12,500	0.20
Independent	12,750	0.21

Source: Data from Roy C. Macridis & Thomas Lancaster (1987). "The Politics of Greece." In Roy C. Macridis (Ed.), *Modern Political Systems: Europe* (338). Englewood Cliffs, New Jersey: Prentice-Hall, Inc.

The transfer of power to PASOK and the essential withering of the centrist parties impacted the organization of the two major political parties. Immediately following 1974, while PASOK succeeded in establishing a well-structured mass organization, New Democracy was organizationally weak. However, after 1981 PASOK "showed symptoms of debilitation of the party apparatus and personnel" (Sotiropoulos, 1996, p. 67). The grassroots organization of PASOK became weaker and conflicts emerged between those at the top of the party hierarchy and local party organizations. Georgios Rallis, Evangelos Averoff-Tossizza, and Constantine Mitsotakis (the successors of Karamanlis) reorganized New Democracy at the local level primarily as a result of the previous election and because they did not have Karamanlis' charisma to be able to control party leaders at the grassroots level. The efforts of New Democracy's leadership were rewarded by an increase in the party membership and by attracting voters from a greater variety of constituencies. New Democracy's efforts, however, have not changed the weak organizational structure of the Greek political parties. But more importantly, the organizational limitations have not reversed democratic consolidation (Morlino, 1995, pp. 347-349).

The victory of Andreas Papandreou in 1981 deepened the consolidation of democracy that had begun under Karamanlis. As Brown (1992) states: "the years 1974 and 1981 were in fact two of the most important in Greek history since the achievement of independence from the Ottoman Empire in 1830. They broke the established historical patterns that had slowed constitutional development and hindered national unity" (p. 44). The elections of 1974 and 1981 changed the pattern of Greek politics that had lasted for about a century. This pattern had resulted from the interaction between the historical political parties, the monarch, the army, foreign powers, the church, a financial oligarchy, and the Greeks of the Diaspora in Western Europe and the United States (Brown, 1992, pp. 44-45).

Since the beginning of the twentieth century, especially since World War II, the political divide was between the royalists and the republicans. After World War II the divide was between the conservatives and the Left. These philosophical and political differences permeated Greek political life. The institution of the monarchy rather than acting as a unifying force became embroiled in politics and aggravated the divisions among the Greeks. The army's role in Greek politics was even greater than that of the monarch. The army's intervention in politics was almost always the rule than the exception. Foreign power interference in the affairs of the Greek state has been constant beginning with the nineteenth century and Greek independence. The Greek Orthodox Church became involved in politics and traditionally supported conservative governments willing to leave its privileges alone. The financial oligarchy has exerted considerable influence on Greek politics. It strongly supported conservative politicians and American interests. The Greeks of the Diaspora in Western Europe played a significant role in securing Greek independence during the nineteenth century. But it was the Greeks of the Diaspora in the United States that have had strong political, economic, and cultural influence in Greece since the end of World War II. Greek-Americans have supported conservative politicians and many were supportive of the 1967-1974 military dictatorship (Brown, 1992, pp. 45-48).

"In terms of Greek political history the promise of PASOK's victory was more in what it symbolized than what it actually was. First of all, it showed that a genuine opposition could come to power without a political or national upheaval. It was a triumph, therefore, for Modern Greek democracy. But even more profound was the fact that it went a long way to bringing the national schism that had characterized twentieth century Greece and which, in the civil war after the Second World War, had become an open and most almost fatal wound" (Brown, 1992, p. 44). The communists were excluded from political life by the right-wing governments from 1949 until 1979 when Karamanlis re-legalized the Communist Party. The left of center forces, by no means communists, were also excluded from power except for a short period between 1963 and 1964 when George Papandreou was the Prime Minister. "Put another way, PASOK's advent on the scene created new political space and provided a suitable institutional vehicle for the incorporation and autonomous participation in the political system of old and new social actors whom the exclusivist system of the postwar period, as it survived down to 1974, had effectively disenfranchised" (Diamantouros, 1991, pp. 25-26). The outcome of the 1981 election also deepened the consolidation of democracy as the opposition party, PASOK, came to power. The transfer of power was peaceful and the outcome represented a break from the uninterrupted dominance of the Right (Gunther, Puhle & Diamantouros, 1995, p. 29). PASOK's victory was the most dramatic breakthrough in the political transformation of Southern Europe in the late 1970s and early 1980s (Petras, Raptis & Sarafopoulos, 1993, p. 161).

On November 22, 1981, Papandreou introduced his program to parliament. According to his program, "national independence, territorial integrity, popular sovereignty and democracy, self-supporting economic and social development, a cultural revival, the revivification of the countryside, the radical improvement of the quality of life in the towns and in the villages, social justice and, finally, social liberation are the targets of our government and set the course we are to follow. The course of change will be a long one" (Kourvetaris & Dobratz, 1987, p. 81). However, the socioeconomic crisis that Papandreou had inherited from the previous government made it difficult to fully implement the policy of *Allaghi*. Although the socialist government liberalized divorce laws, promoted greater equality for women, eliminated the institution of dowry, provided elderly, men, women and farmers with pensions, promoted national reconciliation by recognizing the national resistance and by abolishing the exclusivist and repressive legislation remaining from the 1930s and the period following the Civil War, and established a national health system, much of what Papandreou had been attacking while in opposition remained in place. Unemployment during the first four years of his administration was about 10 percent, the inflation rate was 17-18 percent, investment fell and debt continued to climb. On June 2, 1985, the Greeks went to the ballot box, four months before the four-year parliamentary term had expired. The early elections resulted from the decision be the PASOK leadership to dramatically change its position during the presidential election of March 1985.

Constantine Mitsotakis, New Democracy's new leader since September 1, 1984, supported Karamanlis' candidacy while the communists opposed it. Papandreou on numerous occasions had announced his intention to support the reelection of Karamanlis, but by 1984 he decided to change his position. The two leaders could not agree on the powers of the President of the Republic, Papandreou wished to downgrade the powers of the President (Lane & Ersson, 1994, p. 257). Others believe that Papandreou reversed his position about Karamanlis because 38 percent of PASOK voters viewed the possible alliance with New Democracy in the presidential election as harmful to the country. In addition, the socialists would have lost, they believed, 3-4 percent of their supporters to the communists, which in turn would have cost them their reelection (Demetras, 1991, p. 313). With the passage of time, the PASOK leadership began to claim that Karamanlis represented the establishment and as such would have been a difficult obstacle to overcome in order to implement the radical initiatives of PASOK. However, many of Papandreou's initiatives were moderate and Karamanlis would have not raised any objections. At a later point Papandreou admitted that his decision about Karamanlis was the greatest mistake of his career as a politician (Kariotis, 1992, p. 15).

On March 9, 1985, to the surprise of political analysts, Papandreou proposed the candidacy of Christos Sartzetakis, a judge of the *Areios Pagos*, the Supreme Court. On March 10, Karamanlis resigned and was replaced by Yannis Alevras as acting President. On March 29, after three attempts, the parliament elected Sartzetakis as President. He received 180 of 300 votes, the minimum required number of votes. New Democracy disputed the outcome because the President of parliament, Yannis Alevras, who was the acting President of the Republic, took part in the vote despite the objections of the majority of the constitutional experts (Demetras, 1991, p. 313). A constitutional crisis was averted only because PASOK won the parliamentary elections on June 2, 1985. The victory allowed the government to push through parliament the constitutional amendments regarding the powers of the President (Couloumbis, 1992, p. 91).

With the new President in office, Papandreou decided to exploit his "victory" by calling for early parliamentary elections in June. The elections also resulted from New Democracy's demands for early elections. New Democracy leaders incorrectly believed that Karamanlis' "removal" would upset moderate PASOK supporters, who in turn would vote for the conservatives (Demetras, 1991, p. 314). As the campaign began, both the Communist Party and New Democracy adopted an offensive strategy and attacked PASOK. The communists accused the socialists of failing to fulfill many of their promises and of embracing the practices of the Right of a few decades earlier. The objective of the communists was to prevent PASOK from gaining the required parliamentary majority and compel PASOK to include them in a coalition government to drastically reform Greek society. New Democracy used the slogan *Apallaghi* or disengagement from the politics of PASOK. It emphasized the need for economic reforms, the privatization of the public enterprises, and the necessity to increase domestic and foreign investments. However, disputing the legitimacy of President Sartzetakis, New Democracy had called for his resignation based on how he was elected, proved to be a mistake. It frightened many voters who feared that a constitutional crisis would result from such opposition (Demetras, 1991, p. 314).

While the opposition parties developed an offensive strategy, PASOK adopted a strategy that was defensive and dynamic at the same time. Papandreou's campaign was based on the same themes as before: the continuation of *Allaghi* and the anti-Turkish rhetoric. Papandreou also cultivated the fear that the Right might return to power. PASOK effectively identified the New Democracy of 1985 with the Right of the previous generation, and once again won the elections. Andreas Andrianopoulos, a former New Democracy Minister, asserted that PASOK was the victor because a large percentage of the population resented the old Right. A substantial number of people, 36 percent, stated that one of the reasons they voted for PASOK was to prevent the return of the Right and 21 percent said that that was the only reason they voted as they did (Demetras, 1991, pp. 314-319).

The election, as Table 8 indicates, produced an even greater bipolarization of the party system and caused the total collapse of the Center Union Party.

TABLE 8
Election of June 2, 1985

Political Party	No. of Votes	Percentage
New Democracy	2,599,949	40.84
PASOK	2,916,450	45.82
KKE (Communist Party)	629,518	9.89
All other	314,954	3.45

Source: Data from Thomas Lancaster (1990). "The Politics of Greece." In Roy C. Macridis (Ed.), *Modern Political Systems: Europe* (273). Englewood Cliffs, New Jersey: Prentice Hall.

During Papandreou's second term in office the Greek economy did not perform any better than previously. Growth was slow and the inflation rate in 1987 was as high as 19.3 percent. Papandreou introduced austerity measures to manage the economic problems. The drachma was devalued by about 15 percent, wages were frozen, and stricter exchange controls were established. Despite the ideological and nationalist rhetoric that had helped Papandreou win the 1981 and 1985 elections, the

Prime Minister had to ask the international community for credits, and pragmatic steps were taken to strengthen and modernize the economy. The further removed public opinion was from the traumatic experiences of the 1967-1974 period, the easier it became for Papandreou to moderate his positions about the EEC, NATO, and the United States, and thus approach the international community for assistance (Loulis, Winter 1984-1985, pp. 379-387).

Papandreou's popularity declined even further because of much he had done. He antagonized the religious segment of the Greek population by challenging the Greek Orthodox Church for its political role and its land holdings. Papandreou provoked the opposition of members of the middle- and upper-middle-class Greeks with his decision to nationalize private schools. Many Greeks viewed Papandreou's decision in 1988 to meet the President of Turkey, Ozal, as capitulation. Finally, his decision to divorce his wife of 37 years and to have an affair with a 33-year-old airline stewardess (Lancaster, 1990, pp. 274-275), and the *Koskotas affair*[2] displeased many voters. As Bakatselos (1989) states, the Greek financial and banking system, the sterile political perceptions, and the hypocrisy, led the country to the *Koskotas affair*, and the people to frustration and despair (p. 9).

Papandreou attempted during the last few months before the June 18, 1989, election to rescue PASOK and his government, but allegations of corruption involving him and PASOK Ministers dominated the campaign. Papandreou once again resorted to nationalist and populist themes to attract the support of the voters. As a consequence, domestic issues such as the state of the economy, and educational and civil service reform were completely ignored.

Candidates representing nearly 25 political parties run in the elections of June 18, 1989. One important change was the creation in 1989 of a "leftist front" consisting of nine political parties under the leadership of the communists. This alliance included the Communist Party of the Interior, PASOK dissidents and other left-wing leaders, and it became the third largest political party after PASOK and New Democracy. As Table 9 shows, the elections of June 18, 1989, reintroduced political instability in Greek political life. New Democracy won under 45 percent of the vote and only 144 of 300 seats in parliament. Thus, New Democracy did not gain a majority in parliament. Two weeks after the election a temporary coalition was formed between New Democracy and the "leftist front" with Tzannetakis of New Democracy as Prime Minister. Mr.

Tzannetakis was the first Prime Minister since the fall of the junta in 1974 not to be the leader of a party. The first government of cooperation between the conservatives and the Left in Modern Greek history took the oath of office on July 2, 1989. The new government gave itself three months to "clean up" and democratize public life, and to prepare the country for new elections on November 5, 1989 (Anastasiades, 1993, p. 122). Greece began to enter a new phase in its political life with a coalition government, the first since 1952, which included partners whose hostile relationship went back at least as far as the Civil War.

TABLE 9
Election of June 18, 1989

Political Party	No. of Votes	Percentage
PASOK	2,553,086	39.15
New Democracy	2,885,548	44.25
Communist-Led Coalition	885,564	13.12
Other		3.48

Source: Data from Thomas Lancaster (1990). "The Politics of Greece." In Roy C. Macridis (Ed.), *Modern Political Systems: Europe* (276). Englewood Cliffs, New Jersey: Prentice Hall; To Pontiki (1989). *Oi Ekloges Tes 18es Iouniou 89* (132). Athens: To Pontiki.

PASOK's era in power ended ignominiously after the June 18, 1989, election in an atmosphere characterized by scandals and allegations involving the leadership of the party in cases of fraud, embezzlement, and bribery. Even before the June election, Papandreou's government unsuccessfully endeavored to survive the effects of the *Koskotas affair* and the *purchase of the century*.[3] A great journey, which began in 1974 with the formation of the party and led to the electoral victories in 1981 and 1985, came to an unfortunate end (Lyrintzis, 1993, p. 26).

It could be argued that PASOK's tenure in power was a colossal failure, but that would be an oversimplification. PASOK, during the eight years in power, positively affected Greek politics. "The populist mode of political participation adopted by PASOK had a positive side, to the extent that it incorporated into the political system social strata that were politically marginal during the postwar period" (Lyrintzis, 1993, p. 36). PASOK's eight-year control of the government weakened the traditional cleavages between the communists and the anticommunists, a process, which began under Karamanlis in 1974 and strengthened by PASOK (Lyrintzis, 1993, p. 37). PASOK also developed relatively good relations with the military; promoted decentralization and popular participation; established a national health system; formulated a new electoral law; gained recognition of Greece's special economic position and problems from the EEC; and negotiated an agreement with the United States regarding the military bases in Greece (Kourvetaris & Dobratz, 1987, pp. 88-89).

The Tzannetakis government resigned on October 7, 1989, having completed its work. In the meantime, the members of parliament brought indictments against Mr. Papandreou and four PASOK Ministers. On November 5, the Greeks went to the polls for a second time in 1989 to elect a new parliament. As Table 10 indicates, New Democracy once again received more votes than any other political party, but not enough to form a government by itself. New Democracy added only three seats to its total from the previous election and the "leftist front" lost seven. The real victor was PASOK, which won three extra seats in spite the problems of its leader.

TABLE 10
Election of November 5, 1989

Political Party	No. of Votes	Percentage
New Democracy	3,093,055	46.19
PASOK	2,723,739	40.67
Communist-Led Coalition	734,552	10.97
Other		2.17

Source: Data from G. Anastasiades (1993). *Synchrone Politike Historia Tes Helladas: 1974-1992* (129). Thessaloniki: Malliaris-Paideia A.E.; To Pontiki (1990). *Oi Ekloges Tes 5es Noemvriou 89* (107). Athens: To Pontiki.

After numerous meetings, the leaders of the political parties arrived at an agreement to form a national coalition government. The 85-year old Xenophon Zolotas was chosen as Prime Minister. He was the former director of the Bank of Greece, with prestige inside and outside Greece. The expectations were high, but the government did not succeed in dealing with the serious economic problems. On February 12, 1990, Mitsotakis withdrew from the government the New Democracy Ministers. PASOK and the "leftist front" also behaved similarly. Zolotas considered resigning but did not until the new elections of April 8, 1990.

During the new election campaign, New Democracy based its strategy on the slogans of "new faces" and "new ideas." PASOK called for "revising everything" (Anastasiades, 1993, p. 138). The elections were conducted orderly with the following results:

TABLE 11
Election of April 8, 1990

Political Party	No. of Votes	Percentage
New Democracy	3,088,137	46.89
PASOK	2,543,042	38.61
Communist-Led Coalition	677,059	10.28
Independents	66,801	1.02
Other		3.20

Source: Data from G. Anastasiades (1993). *Synchrone Politike Historia Tes Helladas: 1974-1992* (139). Thessaloniki: Malliaris_Paideia A.E.; To Pontiki (1990). *Oi Ekloges Tes 8es Apriliou 1990* (14). Athens: To Pontiki.

New Democracy captured more votes than in the previous election, but, as in the past, it did not get enough seats in parliament (New Democracy won 150 but needed 151) to form a government by itself. PASOK and the communists lost ground. Constantine Mitsotakis formed a government on April 11, 1990, because the leader of a small Center-Right party (DIANA or Democratic Renewal) declared his intention to support the government with the one Member of Parliament it had elected.

New Democracy returned to power because the experience with the Zolotas government convinced many Greeks of the ineffectiveness of coalition governments; many supporters of PASOK and the communist coalition were dissatisfied with their leaders for participating in the Zolotas government; and none of the small parties presented a credible plan to attract sufficient number of dissatisfied voters (Demetras, 1991, pp. 348-349). The parliamentary elections were followed by the election on May 4, 1990, after two attempts, of Karamanlis as the new President. Karamanlis announced that he had three basic goals: the normal functioning of democracy, the protection of national unity and the tranquility of Greek political life (Anastasiades, 1993, p. 142).

With a one-vote edge in parliament, Prime Minister Mitsotakis needed all the popular support he could muster. Support quickly eroded because of the stiff austerity program, the controversial educational reforms, and the ill-fated attempt to pardon the members of the junta still in prison. Mitsotakis, with little success, tried to justify his policies. He said that austerity was necessary to reduce the $13.8 billion budget deficit, educational reform was needed to conform to the ethics of Greek Orthodox society, and the release of the coup leaders was deemed necessary for humanitarian reasons (*US News & World Report*, 14 January 1991, p. 41).

The Mitsotakis government was even attacked by high-ranking members of New Democracy, critical of the privatization efforts and his foreign policy. New Democracy lost its parliamentary majority (of one vote) because a right-winger decided to sit in parliament as an Independent. This was the latest of a number of defections since Mitsotakis dismissed the former Foreign Minister, Antonis Samaras. Samaras formed his own political party, called Political Spring. He broke away from New Democracy because he thought that any recognition of the word "Macedonia," that is in regards to the Former Yugoslav Republic of Macedonia or FYROM, would legitimize territorial claims by the new state. Samaras asserted that by accepting the name of Former Yugoslav Republic of Macedonia, the government was being too soft and was undermining Greek national interests (*The Economist*, 11 September 1993, p. 53).

Mitsotakis' popularity declined even further, according to public opinion polls down to 27 percent (the lowest of any Greek Prime Minister), because of high unemployment among young Greeks (about 20 percent), the so-called Greek Watergate—an aide to Mitsotakis was accused of bugging the opponents' telephone calls—(*The Economist*, 11 September 1993, p. 53), for giving a Ministry position to his daughter, and for letting his wife meddle in politics. Mitsotakis promised to turn the economy around. But although inflation was the lowest in twenty years, 12.8 percent, GDP growth was about 1 percent. In addition, wages were frozen, government workers were fired, and the gasoline tax was raised by 50 percent. "A lot of Greeks, it is plain, are fed up with three years of austerity" (*The Economist*, 9 October 1993, p. 60). Mitsotakis offered his resignation on September 9, 1993, and called for early elections.

The beneficiary was Andreas Papandreou whose defeat at the previous election seemed to be his last hurrah. PASOK was expected to defeat New Democracy in the elections of October 10, 1993, but not so convincingly (see Table 12). After the election, Miltiadis Evert was chosen to succeed Mitsotakis.

TABLE 12
Election of October 10, 1993

Political Party	No. of Votes	Percentage
PASOK	3,235,017	46.9
New Democracy	2,711,737	39.3
Political Spring	336,460	4.9
Communist Party of Greece	313,001	4.5
Communist-Led Coalition	202,887	2.9
Other		1.5

Source: Data from *The Economist*, 16 October 1993 (57); To Pontiki (1994). *Oi Ekloges Tes 10es Oktovriou 1993* (8-9). Athens: To Pontiki.

Although PASOK officials claimed that the radical days were over, for his cabinet Papandreou chose old associates instead of young party officials. To make matters worse, he appointed his wife as his Chief of Staff. On the economic front, Papandreou resisted privatization of the Greek telecommunications company (OTE) and of the two big oil refineries. Instead, he promised to "undo the wrong committed by the right" (*The Economist*, 16 October 1993, p. 58). He also said that there would be cooperation rather than confrontation with European Union and the United States. However, Greece's adversarial relationship with two of its neighbors, Albania and FYROM, and the state of the Greek economy caused problems with the Europeans and the Americans. "Greece's crumbling economy will add to the friction with the EC. Warnings have already been sounded in Brussels that new measures are needed to stop Greece's budget deficit getting out of control. Unless something is done quickly, this year's government borrowing will reach 14.4% of GDP, almost twice the official forecast of 7.9%" (*The Economist*, 6 November 1993, p. 68).

In 1995, Papandreou's poor health provided PASOK members with the impetus to criticize him and to pressure, to no avail, to step down. In fact, in March 1995, he made sure that his party had a chance to remain in power for the full four-year term by securing the election of Costis Stephanopoulos as President to succeed Karamanlis. Without a new President, the parliament would have been dissolved and the ensuing elections could have caused the defeat of the socialists. On foreign policy, Papandreou was now more inclined than before to improve relations with the European Union, Albania, Turkey, and FYROM (*The Economist*, 25 March 1995, p. 60). However, reform-minded PASOK leaders were growing impatient. They desired a new leadership.

The *gang of four*, as the most important dissidents (Costas Simitis, Vasso Papandreou, Theodoros Pangalos, Paraskevas Avgerinos) became known, were planning to confront Papandreou and compel him to agree on how to proceed in choosing a successor and on the timing of his retirement. Five days before a party meeting, Papandreou was taken to a hospital and his illness convinced the dissidents to temporarily halt their efforts (*The Economist*, 25 November 1995, p. 49). The four, led by Simitis, wanted to strengthen the Greek economy, and improve relations with the Balkan neighbors and the European Union.

The founder of PASOK finally resigned on January 15, 1996, and Costas Simitis was his successor. Mr. Simitis was a founding member of PASOK and held Ministerial positions in Papandreou's governments, but turned against his mentor in 1993 (*Maclean's*, 29 January 1996, p. 25). "Mr. Simitis is bland in comparison with Mr. Papandreou. But that seems to be what Greek voters want" (*The Economist*, 27 January 1996, p. 45). The Greeks, tired of the old politicians, wanted to give him a chance. He is uncharismatic, reliable and moderate, the opposite of Papandreou. Simitis "pledged to introduce a new style of government. This was a tactful reference to Mr. Papandreou's autocratic way of running the country, in which he would personally dictate foreign policy, override the decisions of his economic advisers, and sometimes fire cabinet ministers without warning" (*Europe*, February 1996, p. 9).

Prime Minister Simitis is a technocrat whose "watchword" is caution. He "likes to describe himself as the conductor of an orchestra. . . . He prefers to build consensus within the cabinet and win backing for his policies through persuasion" (*Europe*, October 1997, p. 14). As soon as Mr. Simitis became the Prime Minister he emphasized Greece's obligations in relation to the European Union. Under the direction of Loukas Papademos at the central bank, Yannos Papantoniou at economic planning and Alekos Papadopoulos at finance, the Greek economy, despite the underlying economic problems, began to show signs of life. Inflation was down to 8.1 percent, the deficit fell to 8.9 percent of the GDP and growth was projected to reach 2.8 percent (*The Economist*, 25 Febrauary 1996, pp. 53-54).

Papandreou's resignation was an important development in Modern Greek history. The last of the *old guard* was out of power. He was a charismatic figure who helped guide Greece after the dictatorship and shaped the destiny of Greece for a generation. He was critical of the Americans, but at the end he proved to be an "ally of the United States." "Despite his populist rhetoric, he was, in fact, deeply attached to his American roots, having come to political maturity in the 1960s while teaching economics at Harvard and Berkley. When push came to shove, he neither closed down the US bases, nor pulled Greece out of NATO. Moreover, PASOK, thanks in part to its anti-western bombast, proved to be a center-left bulwark that permanently stunned the growth of the real threat to western interests, the Greek Communist Party" (*New Statesman and Society*, 1996, p. 11).

It did not take long for things to go wrong for Prime Minister Simitis. He had to contend with a confrontation with Turkey over some islands in the Aegean and there was still some infighting among PASOK members. He did not devote the necessary time to the economy and the result was reform delays, an inflation rate of 9 percent, and dimmer hopes for joining economic and monetary union. Yet most of the Greeks liked his performance (*The Economist*, 22 June 1996, p. 50). Greek businessmen were mostly behind him and young voters liked his pro-European views. The West also liked Simitis. Good news for the Prime Minister because he called a snap election on September 22, 1996.

Table 13 shows that the Greek voters decided to elect the sitting Prime Minister.[4] Mr. Simitis defeated New Democracy's Miltiadis Evert who had made many promises to win votes. Mr. Evert promised to restore tax breaks and subsidies to farmers; to abandon PASOK's unpopular new system of taxing the "presumed" rather than the "declared" income of the self-employed, who make about a third of the workforce; to promote the Greek tourist industry; and to quickly implement grants from the European Union (*The Economist*, 14 September 1996, p. 50).

TABLE 13
Election of September 22, 1996

Political Party	No. of Votes	Percentage
PASOK	2,804,404	41.5
New Democracy	2,576,360	38.1
Communists	378,604	5.6
Left Coalition	345,194	5.1
Democratic Renewal	299,392	4.4
Political Spring	198,830	2.9
Others		2.4

Source: Data from *The Economist*, 28 September 1996, p. 60.

With the PASOK members under his control, Simitis demoted many of his rivals but kept them in his government under close "surveillance." He promoted pro-Europeans who had supported him during his rise to power, and he also appointed George Papandreou, the son of Andreas Papandreou, as alternate Foreign Minister. Papandreou became the Foreign Minister of Greece in 1999 when Prime Minister Simitis dismissed Theoforos Pangalos. Papandreou is someone trusted by the United States government, his relationship with the then United States Secretary of State, Madeleine Albright, was good, and he could get along with the former Foreign Minister of Turkey, Tansu Ciller (*The Economist*, 28 September 1996, p. 60), and he is popular with both PASOK factions. Mr. Papandreou is a consensus builder, and an early supporter of Mr. Simitis and his *eksynchtonistes* or modernizers (*The Economist*, 1 May 1999, p. 52).

Delegates to a New Democracy party congress elected Costas Karamanlis, a nephew of Constantine Karamanlis, as their leader hoping that he would lead them back to power. During the reign of Evert, New

Democracy moved to the extreme right and against free enterprise. When elected to the leadership post, Costas Karamanlis was 40 years old without much political experience. He promised to reverse everything, but having the name Karamanlis will not be enough for him to resurrect the party and to defeat the self-modernizing PASOK (*The Economist*, 29 March 1997, pp. 59-60).

With Mr. Simitis as Prime Minister, the image of Greek politics has changed. "For the first time Greece understands that it is part of Europe and that its political and economic success is wholly dependent on the extent to which it chooses to cultivate its relationship with the European Union" (Kurop, 1998, pp. 7-8). The Greek economy has improved dramatically. In order to comply with the terms of the Maastricht Treaty austerity measures were introduced which brought the inflation rate down to about 3 percent, while the growth rate was a healthy 3 percent. Although governmental interference in the economy is still significant, it is understood that interventionism must be replaced by free-market mechanisms. Greece has improved relations with Albania, FYROM, and Bulgaria. Greece became the largest investor in FYROM and Bulgaria, and has signed a 20-year "special ties" agreement with Albania. The distraction remains Greece's relation with Turkey. But even in that front there is an improvement. Former Foreign Minister Pangalos supported Turkey's candidacy for European Union membership in March 1996, when he said that Turkey belongs to Europe (Kurop, 1998, pp. 8-13). Furthermore, Greek and Turkish political leaders have held numerous meetings covering a variety of issues in an attempt to improve relations. For the first time in more than twenty years, Turkish marines landed on Greek territory as part of NATO military exercises. There is guarded optimism even in regards to Cyprus. Recently, the President of Cyprus, Glafcos Clerides, and the Turkish Cypriot leader, Rauf Denktash, met and agreed to begin direct talks in mid January. These developments prompted Prime Minister Simitis to say at a press luncheon, "this development shows that we have succeeded to some degree" (*Athens News Agency Bulletin*, 5 December 2001, p. 1).

Convinced that his party would win a third term in office, the usually cautious Simitis called for new elections for April 9, 2000, six months before he needed to. To his surprise, PASOK won only 43.8 percent of the vote, against 42.7 percent for New Democracy (See Table 14). So why were the Greeks so reluctant to vote for Simitis? His preoccupation with euro membership has prevented him from concentrating on some important social issues. Crime rates are rising, standards are falling in state hospitals, and the country's schools are not as good as they ought to be (*The Economist*, 1 April 2000, p. 50). Although the Greeks seem to be getting tired of PASOK, they are not enthusiastic about the idea of putting the country's fortunes in the hands of the inexperienced Costas Karamanlis. According to a recently published opinion poll, Simitis leads Karamanlis in the category of "most fit for premier" 38.1 percent to 31.9 percent (*Athens News Agency Bulletin*, 5 December 2001, p. 3).

TABLE 14
Election of April 9, 2000

Political Party	No. of Votes	Percentage
PASOK	3,005,162	43.80
New Democracy	2,932,867	42.70
Communist Party of Greece (KKE)	379,116	5.50
Coalition of the Left and Progress Party (SYN)	219,696	3.20
Democratic Social Mevement (DHKKI)	184,373	2.70
Others		2.10

Source: *Athens News Agency Bulletin*, 10 April 2000.
http://www.e-debate.gr/liveelections/site/ekloges2000.asp

The smooth transfer of power from the Right to the Center-Left on October 18, 1981, and the orderly elections of June 2, 1985, June 18, 1989, November 5, 1989, April 8, 1990, October 10, 1993, September 22, 1996 and April 9, 2000, demonstrate the growing maturity of the Greek political system, and "the capacity of newly-founded institutions to absorb political change" (Ioakimidis, 1984, p. 58).

Democracy and the Domestic Environment

The transition from authoritarianism to democracy as well as the consolidation of democracy was unexpectedly brief.[5] Greece has undergone many changes since 1974 and a number of reasons, domestic as well as external, have contributed to the consolidation of democracy. Domestic forces and calculations have much contributed to the consolidation of democracy. The small number of lower echelon officers involved in the 1967 coup meant that they did not pose great threat to the civilian government after 1974. Also, despite the brutality of the dictatorship, the gradualist and cautious approach of Karamanlis in dealing with those responsible for violence against the people of Greece made reaction from their supporters against the civilian government difficult (Schmitter, 1991, pp. 5-6). The army, of course, remains an important player, but its political role appears to have been minimized, if not ended. No significant domestic actors, in an attempt to achieve their objectives, call for a military coup anymore.

But among the domestic forces, what is the most important reason for the consolidation of democracy is the strength of civil society.[6] "For political democracy to become and remain an alternative mode of political domination, a country must possess a civil society in which certain community and group identities exist independent of the state and in which certain types of self-constituted units are capable of acting autonomously in defense of their own interests and ideals. Moreover, these identities and interests must not only be dispersed through out the country, they most also be capable of being concentrated when the occasion demands, that is, they must be organized for coherent collective action. In democracies, such participation is accomplished in large part consensually through political parties which compete to win electoral majorities, ally with others in dominant coalitions, or enter into consociational arrangements" (Schmitter, 1991, p. 6).

A strong civil society serves democracy by: providing the basis for limiting the power of the state; stimulating political participation; contributing to the development of tolerance, moderation, willingness to compromise and respect for different points of view; creating other avenues for the articulation, aggregation and presentation of interests; training political leaders; disseminating information; and promoting freedom of association (Diamond, 1996, pp. 230-234). One indicator of the strength of civil society is that after 1974 "monarchic oligarchy without the colonels in Greece is simply not a viable option" (Schmitter, 1991, p. 7). Another indicator is the nature of the political parties that have emerged after the fall of the junta in 1974. Greece has a relatively stable multiparty system sustained by electoral and administrative systems, which rest on legal guarantees. These parties provide identification for the voter, express interests and they check each other (Lipset, 1998, pp. 5-8).

Personalistic and charismatic politics is not as important anymore, the Communist Party is more moderate in its strategy, extreme right wing political parties have virtually ceased to exist, and all major political actors have accepted "the rules of the game." In addition, the two major political parties, PASOK and New Democracy, have moved to the center. Karamanlis and Papandreou "broke with tradition on the right and center and transformed their parties into center-right and center-left" (Mavrogordatos, 1983b, p. 82). These parties have become catch-all parties, appealing to those in the middle of the ideological spectrum. Presently, there is sufficient consensus regarding a number of important issues ranging from the economy to the welfare state, education, European Union membership, and NATO. It would be a serious mistake to underestimate the stabilizing role of PASOK and New Democracy (Loulis, 1995, p. 541).

In addition, the high turnover in Members of Parliament (MPs) since the rise of PASOK has created a climate that is more supportive of democratic consolidation (Pridham, 1990, p. 240). This has been enhanced by the greater number of younger deputies elected (see Table 15) since 1974.

TABLE 15
Age Distribution of Members of Parliament

Age	1964		1974		1977		1981		1985	
group	No.	%	No.	%	No.	%	No.	%	No.	%
25-9	1	0.3	7	2.3	3	1.0	6	2.0	1	0.3
30-9	25	8.3	45	5.0	57	19.0	51	17.0	30	10.0
40-9	65	21.6	78	26.0	95	31.6	115	38.3	102	34.0
50-9	120	40.0	83	27.6	68	22.6	68	22.6	91	30.3
60-9	68	22.6	71	23.6	56	18.6	42	14.0	59	19.6
70+	21	7.0	15	5.0	18	6.0	18	6.0	17	5.6
Not avail.			1	0.3	3	1.0				

Source: Data from N. Alivizatos (1990). "The difficulties of 'rationalization' in a polarized political system: the Greek Chamber of Deputies." In U. Liebert & M. Cotta (Eds.), *Parliament and Democratic Consolidation in Southern Europe: Greece, Italy, Portugal, Spain and Turkey* 138. London & New York: Pinter Publishers.

The experience of 1967-1974 convinced many Greeks that political modernization was a necessity (Ioakimides, 1984, pp. 44-45). Often it is said that the "Greeks, . . . , are wonderful patriots but terrible citizens. They have a highly developed sense of national identity but almost no sense of responsibility towards the state they live in" (*The Economist*, 22 May 1993, p. 17). The Greeks blame their "unkind" history for this. For very few years since independence from the Ottomans have the Greeks felt in control of their country. Their nineteenth century kings were from northern Europe, they have experienced military dictatorships, the Germans occupied them during World War II, the United States rebuilt them after 1945, and then the Western Europeans came back in the form of the European Community and its money (*The Economist*, 22 May 1993, p. 17). "History, in short, . . . , has until now discouraged the Greeks from learning the proper relationship between the citizen and the democratic state" (*The Economist*, 22 May 1993, p. 17).

History has turned "kind" again. The majority of the Greeks are now strong supporters of democratic principles. The Greeks have "matured politically as a result of the harsh experiences of the seven-year dictatorship" (Papacosma, 1983, p. 38). The Greeks now view their democracy as legitimate, and as Morlino and Montero (1995) state, "ultimately, democratic legitimacy is based on the belief that for that particular country at that particular juncture no other type of regime could assure a more successful pursuit of collective goals" (p. 233). The major actors in the political system (political parties, interests groups, unions, business, military) view democratic processes as the "only game in town" (Lipset, 1998, p. 8).

Democracy requires a culture supportive of democracy. Presently in Greece the citizenry and the political elites have accepted the principles underlying freedom of speech, media, and assembly. As Table 16 indicates, among the Southern European countries the highest percentage of positive attitudes toward democracy is found in Greece. In addition, the Greeks believe that today there are no alternatives to the present democratic system. Furthermore, as Table 17 demonstrates, the severe economic problems that have faced all Southern European countries, including Greece, during the 1980s and early 1990s have not diminished support for democracy.

TABLE 16
Attitudes of Southern Europeans Towards Democracy Expressed in 1985

	Portugal	Spain	Italy	Greece
Diffuse Legitimacy				
Democracy always preferable	61%	70%	70%	87%
Authoritarianism preferable in some cases	9%	10%	13%	5%
All the same	7%	9%	10%	6%
"Don't know" or no answer	23%	11%	7%	2%
Opinions on the Past				
Bad	30%	28%	37%	59%
Part good, part bad	42%	44%	43%	31%
Good	13%	17%	6%	6%
"Don't know" or no answer	15%	11%	14%	4%
Perceived Efficacy				
Our Democracy works well	5%	8%	4%	35%
Many defects, but it works	63%	60%	61%	46%
Getting worse and will not Work at all	11%	20%	28%	14%
"Don't know" or no answer	21%	11%	6%	4%

Source: Data from L. Morlino & J.R. Montero (1995). "Legitimacy and Democracy in Southern Europe." In R. Gunther, N.P. Diamantouros, & H.J. Puhle (Eds.), *The Politics of Democratic Consolidation: Southern Europe in Comparative Perspective* 236. Baltimore & London: The Johns Hopkins University Press.

TABLE 17
Preferences for Democracy over Authoritarianism in European Community Countries, 1992

	Prefer Democracy	Prefer Authoritarianism	"They're All the Same"	"Don't know," No Answer
Denmark	92%	4%	2%	1%
Greece	90%	4%	3%	2%
Portugal	83%	9%	4%	4%
Luxembourg	82%	2%	6%	9%
Germany	81%	8%	7%	3%
(West Germany	83%	8%	5%	2%)
Netherlands	81%	9%	5%	5%
Spain	78%	9%	7%	6%
France	78%	7%	11%	5%
United Kingdom	76%	6%	11%	6%
Italy	73%	14%	6%	7%
Belgium	70%	10%	10%	10%
Ireland	63%	10%	21%	6%
EC average	78%	9%	8%	5%

Source: Data from L. Morlino & J.R. Montero (1995). "Legitimacy and Democracy in Southern Europe." In R. Gunther, N.P. Diamantouros, & H.J. Puhle (Eds.), *The Politics of Democratic Consolidation: Southern Europe in Comparative Perspective* 238.
Baltimore & London: The Johns Hopkins University Press.

Finally, Table 18 demonstrates that throughout the 1980s and early 1990s the Greeks were comparable to other Western Europeans regarding their satisfaction with the performance of their own governments.

TABLE 18
Satisfaction with How Democracy Works

	1985	1987	1989	1991	1993
Portugal	34%	70%	60%	70%	54%
Spain	51%	55%	60%	61%	39%
Italy	28%	26%	27%	33%	32%
Greece	51%	49%	52%	37%	45%
European Community	58%	57%	66%	57%	41%

Source: Data from L. Morlino & J.R. Montero (1995). "Legitimacy and Democracy in Southern Europe." In R. Gunther, N.P. Diamantouros, & H.J. Puhle (Eds.), *The Politics of Democratic Consolidation: Southern Europe in Comparative Perspective* 239. Baltimore & London: The Johns Hopkins University Press.

Democracy and the United States

The United States has also contributed to the consolidation of democracy in Greece. During and after the Greek Civil War, the United States was sympathetic to the forces of the Center and the Left. In fact, the government of the United States was enthusiastic with the success of the Center and the Left in the elections of 1950. United States policy was dramatically altered with the Korean War. The war in the Korean peninsula convinced the policy makers in Washington that the Soviet danger was a military one and that its confrontation had to be based not on political and economic reforms through the Center and the Left, but it had to be based on military elements with military as well as political responsibilities (Goldbloom, 1976, pp. 348-349). The United States began to consistently support financially and militarily the conservative Right. Greece became dependent upon the United States for assistance, and the United States played an influential role in Greek domestic and international affairs.

After the fall of the junta and the invasion of Cyprus by Turkey in 1974, Greek governments, who believed that the Americans had sponsored the 1967 coup, re-evaluated and redefined the relationship with the United States. The objective was to change the relationship from a hierarchical to a balanced one by entering the European Community and by becoming less dependent on the United States. The outcome of these efforts has been an asymmetrical interdependence because the United States is still the one actor that can determine and safeguard the balance of power between Greece and Turkey (Ifantis, 1996, pp. 148-149). Furthermore, the relationship between the two countries is asymmetrical for many reasons including the fact that the United States is the only remaining military and economic superpower. Even though American political influence in Greece has declined, the relationship with the United States remains important as evidenced by the recent (January 2002) meeting between Prime Minister Simitis and President Bush in Washington, D.C. More importantly, the United States advanced the interests of Greek democracy when it was decided that authoritarianism in Greece was not a viable option (Schmitter, 1991, pp. 4-5).

Democracy and the European Community/ European Union

One of the most important reasons for the consolidation of democracy was and is the supportive environment in Europe. "Greece has become enmeshed in a complex network of regional institutions, commercial exchanges, political pressures, party linkages, treaty obligations, citizen contacts, and normative expectations that reward conformity to democracy and punish transgressions from it" (Schmitter, 1991, p. 4). Democratization was a requirement that had to be satisfied for Greece to join the European Community in 1981. European Community/European Union membership "encourages and in certain ways compels the opening up of systems to new institutionalized forms of external cooperation. It requires governmental and administrative structures to adapt to regular procedures at the European level. Political leaders (notably cabinet ministers) are drawn into the functioning of the different versions of the council of ministers; national officials from a wide variety of ministries are involved in the EC's routinized form of diplomacy; and new and old member states alike take their turns in managing the EC presidency, which involves an intense effort in political initiative and statecraft as well as an administrative burden. The pressures on political elites to adopt a 'European' approach are considerable, especially during service in the EC presidency" (Pridham, 1995, p. 180).

There is no doubt that European Community/European Union membership has assisted democratic consolidation and stabilization. Not every scholar, of course, agrees with this conclusion. For example, Mouzelis states, ". . . one basic weakness of our democratic system is that for various-primarily historical-reasons, civil society is exceptionally anemic. This weakness takes the shape of an arbitrary despotic state and of a political system held hostage by the political parties . . ." (Ioakimidis, 1998, p. 203). Legg and Roberts (1997) go even further by saying that Greece is destined to remain a country on the periphery within the European Union because of the "perpetual imbalance between the state and civil society" (pp. 5-6).

But for numerous reasons civil society has recently gained strength. Diamantouros (1997) argues that the cumulative effect of important reforms in the state-controlled sector, the self-employed sector, education, mass media and political parties ". . . will be the empowerment of Greek civil society to change its traditional patterns of interaction with the state. The adoption of universalistic logics in the formation of public policies can help generate new and more durable solidaristic arrangements within society. These arrangements can, in turn, enhance the legitimacy of the state and contribute to the gradual erosion of the culture of cynicism and distrust in state-society relations that is the major long-term legacy of particularism in modern Greece" (Diamantouros, 1997, p. 37). Greece's European Union membership has strengthened civil society by: consolidating democracy; weakening the role and control of the state over society, and the parallel strengthening of social institutions and ultimately civil society; and the introduction of new rights for the citizens (Ioakimidis, 1998, pp. 205-212).

The establishment of democracy was viewed as necessary in order to secure financial assistance from the European Community/European Union (Huntington, 1996, p. 5). Membership has facilitated modernization and has compelled Greek governments to bring down inflation and budget deficits (Dunphy, 1995, p. 143), hence strengthen the Greek economy. During the 1960s the Greek economy was considered a "miracle," but until recently it was considered an "antimiracle." The growth of Greek domestic product (see Table 19) had suffered a chronic decline for many years and, at the same time, the proportions of domestic product devoted to public and private invested had also declined (Thomadakis, 1995, p. 102).

TABLE 19
Growth and Investment Rates

Years	Growth Rate of GDP	Private Investment to GDP	Public Investment to GDP
1961-65	7.8	16.2	7.7
1966-70	6.7	19.3	7.7
1971-75	5.7	18.9	8.0
1976-80	4.2	17.5	5.4
1981-85	1.5	13.0	6.3
1986-90	1.8	12.5	4.9

Source: Data from Stavros B. Thomadakis (1995). "The Greek Economy and European Integration: Prospects for Development and Threats of Underdevelopment." In Dimitri Constas & Theofanis G. Stavrou (Eds.), *Greece Prepares for the Twenty-first Century* 103. Baltimore & London: The Johns Hopkins University Press.

Since 1990, Greece has been successful in placing its public finances in order. The budget deficit has come down from twenty percent to eight percent of gross domestic product (Keridis, 1997, p. 85

The expectation among many Greeks is that the Community will promote Greece's security and economic development (Verney, 1987, p. 268).[7] In addition, European Union membership has been used as a diplomatic lever and has acted as a restraining agent. Greece has used its membership to pressure Turkey and FYROM to modify their behavior and claims. In turn, the European Union has restrained Greece with respect to Turkey and FYROM (Couloumbis & Yannas, 1996, p. 163). As Russett and Oneal state (2001), "International organizations may reduce the likelihood of conflict in various ways. They may directly coerce and restrain those who break the peace, serve as agents of mediation and arbitration, or reduce uncertainty in negotiations by conveying information. They may encourage states to expand their conception of the interests at stake, promoting more inclusive and longer-term thinking; shape general norms and principles of appropriate behavior; or encourage empathy and mutual identification among peoples" (p. 37). Thus, European Union membership represents acceptance of the democratic credentials of Greece and offers a guarantee against a return to the dictatorial past (Pridham, 1995, p. 175).

Conclusion

From the early nineteenth century to 1974, Greece was a client of Great Powers. Powers such as England, France, Russia, and the United States (the patrons) frequently intervened in the affairs of Greece, and as a consequence the Westphalian and domestic sovereignty of Greece was also compromised. It is correct to argue that foreign intervention made possible the creation of the Modern Greek nation-state. The Greek revolution against the Ottomans, which led to an independent Greece, would not have succeeded without assistance from the Great European Powers of the period. Foreign advice, as well as economic and military assistance, in various ways strengthened the modern state. But it is also correct to say that by violating Greek sovereignty, the Great Powers weakened the state. The institution of the monarchy was imposed upon the Greeks, which often brought misfortune. Furthermore, foreign interference played a crucial role regarding calamities such as the *Ethnikos Dikhasmos*, the *Ethnike Catastrophe*, the Civil War, and even the military dictatorship of 1967-1974. Because of these bitter and humiliating experiences, many Greeks considered much of their modern history as "unkind," and developed a mindset that was defensive, resistant to change, and conducive to blaming the external environment for many of the problems confronting them (Pettifer, 1996. p. 19).

Circumstances and the environment began to change in 1974. Greece became democratic, and relations with the United States and European powers were transformed. As pointed out earlier, the Greeks consider democracy to be "the only game in town," and they believe their more recent history has turned "kind" again. Greek governments have welcomed more opportunities to participate in multinational efforts, i.e., Bosnia, Yugoslavia and Afghanistan. The Greek government, especially under the tutelage of Prime Minister Simitis as well as Foreign Minister George Papandreou, has emphasized not only the responsibilities of other governments and institutions toward Greece, but also the responsibilities of Greece toward these governments and institutions including the European Union.

Numerous asymmetries (economic, military, etc.) remain between Greece and the United States as well as most individual European Union members, and as a consequence Greece is still their client. Even though a client, Greece has derived many benefits especially from its European Union membership. Administrative, political, and economic reforms have been enacted in order to meet European Union requirements. Public discourse often is dominated by reform related concerns. Greek foreign policy has become less adventurous, more pro-West, and more moderate. Furthermore, although Westphalian sovereignty is still being compromised, the domestic sovereignty of Greece has been strengthened by the improved and more responsible relationship with the United States and the European Union. The financial, military, political, and diplomatic support that Greece receives from its patrons has enhanced the effectiveness of the Greek state to maintain control within its boundaries, and has thus even more legitimized the state.

Greece joined the European Community in 1981, and since 1993 has been a member of the European Union. At first, from 1981 to 1985, Greece was a "reluctant" member, was viewed as obstructive, irresponsible, and even referred to as the "sick man of Europe." Greece was often criticized for not abiding by European Union rules and for adopting positions outside European Union consensus (Featherstone, 1996, pp. 6-7). In June 1995, the then Prime Minister of Greece, Andreas Papandreou, declared that Greece "was a stranger within the European Union" after he had met with his colleagues at the European Council of Cannes. His declaration was a demonstration of his frustration that resulted from the fact that the French Prime Minister, Jacques Chirac, had criticized Greece for breaking ranks with the European Union members and for imposing a trade embargo against FYROM (Axt, 1997, p. 9). Thanks to the decision by the leadership of the major political parties to support the Europeanization effort and to accept "the European logic," Greece has become a more cooperative and contributing member. The Greek government has become more assertive, in a constructive way, and wishes to project an image of a partner within the European Union rather than a client. As Demetrokalles says: "we must endeavor to make Greece stronger, respected and credible in relationship to friends and foes. We must not continue to play the role of the subjugated anymore" (p. 128).

According to Greece's Balkan envoy, Alex Rondos, for many years, Greece was on the wrong side of every policy issue, and the West considered the Greeks as miscreants. The Greek government had a knack for choosing the wrong friends and annoying its allies in NATO and the European Union. That was the old Greece. The new Greece under Prime Minister Simitis and Foreign Minister George Papandreou has adopted a much different approach to relations with various countries. Both were educated in the West, they are modernist and Europe-oriented, and they seek to make Greece a more dynamic democracy and a force of stability in the region (Ernsberger & Vlahou, 2002).

Before departing for the United States in early January 2002, Prime Minister Costas Simitis told members of the press of his government's plans for Greece's "constructive presence in the EU." He also stated that Greece "had proved it was a country that participated on an equal footing in the European Union and was actively involved in forming the developments." More specifically, the Prime Minister said: "Greece is dynamically standing out as a country of stability. From our privileged position, we are able to contribute to peace and prosperity in our neighborhood and more broadly, indeed in an area that is faced with crises and conflicts. . . . Our effort must be directed particularly towards wiping out friction spots at the regional level and in the comprehensive reinforcement of the country at international level. Greece has a special responsibility towards the peoples and countries of the region to consolidate the principles of peace, international law and cooperation and advance them in every direction" (*Athens News Agency Bulletin*, 9 January 2002, p. 1).

Greece has improved its relationship not only with the United States and the European Union, but also with its Balkan neighbors and Turkey. According to research published by the Rand National Security Research Division, "Greece has been profoundly affected by recent changes in the international environment, on its borders, and within the country itself. Greece has become progressively more modern and more European, and its international policy has become more sophisticated. . . . The geopolitical scene has evolved in ways that present new challenges and new opportunities for Athens in its relations with Europe, the United States, and its neighboring countries" (*Athens News Agency Bulletin*, p. 6). Greece, being a member of the European Union and a Balkan country, has an important role to play. Greece maintains good relations with Bulgaria, Croatia, Slovenia, Bosnia-Herzegovina, the Federal Republic of

Yugoslavia, and Romania. Even though some outstanding issues remain, Greece's relationship with Albania and FYROM has dramatically improved (Kourvetaris, 1999, pp. 412-413). In fact, there has been such a turn-around in the relationship between these three countries, Greece could be considered as Albania's and FYROM's patron. There have been numerous meetings at the highest levels involving the three governments. Furthermore, Greece is one of the largest investors in both Albania and FYROM.

Greece, Foreign Minister Papandreou said, is "encouraging human and minority rights in southeastern Europe, democratization of institutions, good-neighborly relations and the inviolability of borders. . . . The priorities now . . . are to secure permanent peace by resolving bilateral issues; to give new democracies permanency by building strong institutions guaranteeing the rule of law; to contain and eradicate organized crime; to turn opportunistic capital investment into permanent business ventures providing youth with the prospect of a secure future; and to turn segregated communities into multi-cultural societies by investing in education" (*Athens News Agency Bulletin*, 30 November 2001, pp. 1-2).

During the civil war in Yugoslavia over Kosovo, Greek public opinion was pro-Serb. At the beginning of the Kosovo conflict in 1999, the Greek government was concerned about refugees and the reaction of its own people, and attempted to persuade the allies not to bomb the Serbs. Simultaneously, the Greek government refused to break ranks with NATO. Presently, Greece has a small number of peacekeepers in Bosnia and Kosovo. Furthermore, under a Greek Plan for Economic Reconstruction in the Balkans, $586 million has been pledged to Albania, FYROM, Bulgaria, and Romania (Ernsberger & Vlahou, 2002, p. 3).

Through out the Cold War years and until very recently, relations between Greece and Albania were tense. One of the major issues was the treatment of ethnic Greeks in Albania. The Greek government believes they were mistreated because of their Orthodox faith. Many Albanians have illegally crossed the border into Greece. Albanians work in menial jobs, and are thought of being involved in robberies and murders. However, relations between the two neighbors have improved. Greece has signed numerous agreements with Albania covering economic, educational, military, and police matters. Greece provides development assistance to Albania. Over 120 Greek companies operate in Albania creating more than 5,000 jobs. Greece has a military unit in Albania as part of the multinational force stationed to maintain order there. Finally, Greek

Orthodox people in Albania are once again free to practice their faith (Kourvetaris, 1999, pp. 414-415).

The disintegration of the Soviet Union and the revolutions in Eastern Europe, have changed the political landscape in the Balkans. Yugoslavia has given way to the new nation-states of Croatia, Slovenia, and the Former Yugoslav Republic of Macedonia (FYROM). The birth of FYROM generated a conflict with Greece. Even though the Greek government recognizes the people of the former Yugoslav republic of Macedonia, it objects to the use of the name Macedonia. Greece objects to the use of the Vergina star (a sixteen-point star associated with King Philip of ancient Macedonia). In addition, the Greek government believes that FYROM has expansionist aims. Despite the recent past, there has been a dramatic improvement regarding relations between the two countries (Kourvetaris, 1999, pp. 413-414). When fighting with Albanian guerrillas erupted last spring, Greece came to the assistance of its foe. At the insistence of Foreign Minister Papandreou, FYROM's Foreign Minister flew to Tirana prompting the government of Albania to disavow the rebels. Greece helped to set up refugee camps in both countries. Today, Greece is FYROM's largest trading partner. There are plans to build an oil pipeline between the two countries. Greek companies have invested about $400 million-making FYROM the biggest recipient of Greek direct investment (Ernsberger & Vlahou, 2002). FYROM's Prime Minister, Ljubco Georgievski, said, "his country needs a kind of economic assistance and customs union with Greece and a cultural rapprochement and that such a thing will help the speedy opening of his country's doors to the European Union." He also said, "if Greek capital had not infiltrated last year his country would have gone bankrupt" (*Athens News Agency Bulletin*, 2 January 2002, pp. 3-4).

The best news is the encouraging signs of rapprochement between Greece and Turkey. Last year after a devastating earthquake, Greece came to the assistance of Turkey. Two years ago Foreign Minister Papandreou was welcomed by students at the Middle East Technical University in Ankara where he took numerous questions from students-the first visit to Turkey by a Greek Foreign Minister in 27 years. Papandreou and his counterpart, Ismail Cem, talked regularly and have a good relationship. Mr. Papandreou recalled that two years ago he and Mr. Cem had expressed the hope of better bilateral relations which "history seemed to have frozen into a constant rivalry and conflict." Now, two years later, Papandreou said, he needed to express not only hope but also "significant progress" (*Athens News Agency Bulletin*, 30 November 2001, p. 2).

There are numerous disputes between Greece and Turkey including territorial waters, the Aegean Sea continental shelf, airspace over the Aegean, and the fortification of the Aegean islands. Greece would like to extend its territorial waters from six to twelve miles. Turkey has extended its territorial waters in the Black Sea and along its southern coast. The Turkish government, however, refuses to recognize Greece's right to do the same in the Aegean and has threatened war if Greece exercises its right. While the Greeks think that the Aegean continental shelf is an extension of the Greek mainland and island coasts of Greece, the Turks believe that the continental shelf is an extension of Anatolia and deny the continental shelf for the Greek islands. The Aegean airspace consists of two issues: a. the Greek national airspace and b. the Athens FIR (Flight Information Regions). When in 1931 Greece adopted a 10-mile national airspace, Turkey and other governments did not raise any objections. Since the establishment of the International Civil Aviation Organization (ICAO) in 1949 and the Athens FIR, traffic through the Aegean airspace follows the 10-mile zone as Greece's national airspace. In August of 1974, the Turkish government issued a warning to aviators claiming that its own FIR extended as far as the middle of the Aegean, a region that includes many Greek islands. The Treaty of Lausanne (1923) called for the partial demilitarization of some of Eastern Aegean islands. In addition, the Treaty of Paris (1947) stipulated the total demilitarization of the Dodecanese Islands. Much has changed since 1923 and 1947. Turkey has had an expansionist posture in the Aegean, and in 1974 Turkish troops invaded Cyprus and still occupy approximately 30 percent of the island. The Greeks argue that they must fortify the island to defensive purposes (Kourvetaris, 1999, pp. 403-410).

For many years there was a basic disagreement between the governments of the two countries regarding the above-mentioned disputes. While the Turkish government wanted to resolve the disputes through bilateral negotiations, the Greek government wished to utilize international organizations and institutions such as the United Nations and the International Court of Justice. The Greek Foreign Minister announced that Greece and Turkey would begin negotiations to reach a compromise formula to take the Aegean Sea continental shelf to the International Court of Justice. Furthermore, the Turkish Foreign Minister announced that Turkey accepts the European Union's "Agenda 2000" proposals, including recourse to the International Court of Justice, as well as United Nations Resolution 33 for the resolution of Aegean differences (*Athens News Agency Bulletin*, 29 January 2002, pp. 1-2).

As for Cyprus, which brought Greece and Turkey close to war numerous times since the island gained its independence from Great Britain in 1960, Turkey's policy has been consistent since the 1974 invasion of the island. But even in regards to Cyprus, there are reasons to be optimistic. During early December 2001, the Greek and Turkish Cypriot leaders, Glafcos Clerides and Rauf Denktash, met face-to-face for the first time in four years. The Turkish Cypriot proposed "negotiations for the settlement of the Cyprus dispute, starting in mid-January, should continue without a break and aim for a settlement by June." Prime Minister Simitis applauded the meeting and expressed optimism. He said, "this development shows that we have succeeded to some degree" (*Athens News Agency Bulletin*, 5 December 2001, p. 1). About 300 Greek and Turkish Cypriot leaders held their first bi-communal meeting of the New Year during the first week of January at the Ledra Palace Hotel in the Nicosia buffer zone. They "expressed their common wish for a settlement as soon as possible" (*Athens News Agency Bulletin*, 7 January 2002, p. 4).

Notes

Introduction

1. For further understanding of sovereignty read: James A. Caporaso (Summer 2000). Changes in the Westphalian Order: Territory, Public Authority, and Sovereignty. *International Studies Review, 2* (2), 1-28; Kathryn Hochstetler, Ann Marie Clark, & Elisabeth J. Friedman (December 2000), Sovereignty in the Balance: Claims and Bargains at the UN Conferences on the Environment, Human Rights, and Women. *International Studies Quarterly, 44* (4), 591-614; Bruce Bueno de Mesquita (2000). Popes, Kings, and Endogenous Institutions: The Concordat of Worms and the Origins of Sovereignty. *International Studies Review, 2* (2), 93-118.

2. A substantial work on patron-client relationships is: Steffen W. Schmidt, James C. Scott, Carl Lande, & Laura Guasti (Eds.). (1977). *Friends, Followers, and Factions*. Berkeley, Los Angeles: University of California Press.

Chapter 1

1. The *Megali Idea*, or Great Idea, which became the dominant ideology from the inception of the Modern Greek nation-state to 1922, was an attempt to create a sense of loyalty to the state. But even the *Megali Idea* was a by-product of the policies of the Protecting Powers. England, France and Russia, in the early nineteenth century, wanted to maintain the status quo as much as possible and for that purpose they "carved out a diminutive Greece which included barely one-quarter of all Greeks living in the eastern Mediterranean" (Papacosma, 1983, p. 31). The borders of Greece, established by the 1832 treaty of London, ran from the Gulf of Arta to the Gulf of Lamia. Beyond these frontiers were Epirus, Thessaly and Macedonia where many Greeks lived who wanted to be part of the new kingdom (Tatsios, 1984, p. 5). Those who advanced the *Megali Idea* aspired to liberate all territories once considered Greek and to unite them into a single state with Constantinople as its capital. "It has been said that, until a nation has completely vindicated its right to exist, it is hard for it to settle down and make its life worth living" (Tatsios, 1984, p. 6).

2. During Holy Week in 1849 a member of the Rothschild family was visiting Athens and the government decided, as a courtesy to the Jewish visitor, to ban the custom of burning Juntas in effigy. The people ignored the government orders and the police resorted to force. During the fighting the house of a Portuguese known as Don Pacifico was destroyed. Palmerston, the Prime Minister of England, argued that Don Pacifico was entitled to "her Majesty's protection" because he was born in Gibraltar. Ignoring the advice of Queen Victoria, Palmerston ordered a blockade of Greece, a blatant example of gunboat diplomacy. The matter was settled at a small fraction of Don Pacifico's demands and the blockade was lifted twenty-two days later (Kousoulas, 1974, pp. 28-29).

Chapter 3

1. EAM, communist dominated, was established in 1941 to resist the Germans and provide social services. It dominated the country from 1943 to 1944 and became a powerful party in 1945. It was weakened thereafter as a result of right-wing persecution and faded away in 1947. ELAS was established in 1942 and was the armed force of *EAM*. After its defeat by the British and Greek troops in December 1944, ELAS was disbanded according to the *Varkiza* agreement of February 1945. EDES was the main anti-Communist resistance organization and an instrument of the British (Close, 1995, pp. Xii-xiii).

2. Seeking the support of highly placed patrons was a means for the Greeks during the years of Ottoman occupation to protect themselves. Patron/client relationships survived after independence, and persist even today. The patron helps the clients to find jobs and to mediate with a state bureaucracy that is inefficient. In return the patrons expect their clients to support them, including voting for them if involved in politics. One of the outcomes of clientilism is *rouspheti* and *mesa*. *Rouspheti* means the reciprocal dispensation of favors, and *mesa*, the means or connections that are indispensable in daily life (Clogg, 1992, pp. 3-4; Campbell, 1983, p. 195).

Chapter 5

1. According to J.J. Linz, A. Stephan & R. Gunther (1995) "democratic transitions relate to the creation of democratic regimes in which there is open contestation for the right to win control of the government, and this in turn requires free elections, the results of which determine who governs. (p. 78); Morlino (1987) says that "the transition begins when the political and civil rights that characterize any liberal-democratic arrangement begin to gain open recognition and several formal and actual constraints on the manifestations of political pluralism are overcome" (P. 54).

2. George Koskotas, a banker and a media mogul, was arrested on October 20, 1988, for embezzling $200 million from the Bank Crete, of which he was chairman (Kariotis, p. 25).

3. The *purchase of the century* refers to the purchase of fighter planes from the United States and France worth billions of dollars (Kariotis, 1992, p. 25).

4. Greek Prime Ministers (1843-Present)

Prime Ministers after the Constitution of 1843

Andreas Metaxas 1843-1844
Alex. Mavrokordatos 1844
Ioannis Kolettis 1844-1847
Kitsos Tzavellas 1847-1848
G. Kountouriotis 1848
Konstant. Kanaris 1848-1849, 1865
Anton. Kriezis 1849-1854
Dim. Voulgaris 1855-1857, 1862-1867, 1866, 1871, 1874
Athan. Miaoulis 1857-1862
Ioannis Kolokotronis 1862
Zinovios Valvis 1863, 1864
Diomidis Kyriakos 1863
Benizelos Roufos 1863, 1865
Alex. Koumoundouros 1865-1866, 1870, 1875, 1876, 1877, 1878, 1880
Epamein. Deligeorgis 1865-1870, 1872, 1876, 1877
Aristeidis Moraitinis 1867-1868
Thrasyvoulos Zaimis 1869-1870, 1871
Charilaos Trikoupis 1875-1878, 1880, 1882, 1892, 1893
Theodoros Diligianis 1885-1890, 1895
Dim. Valvis 1886
Kon. Konstantopoulos 1892
Sot. Sotiropoulos 1893
Nikol. Deligiannis 1895
Dimitrios Rallis 1897-1905, 1906
Alex. Zaimis 1897-1899, 1915
Georg. Theotokis 1899-1903, 1905, 1908
Kyriak. Mavromihahis 1909-1910
Stef. Dragoumis 1910
Elef. Venizelos 1910-1915, 1917-1920, 1928-1932
Dim. Gounaris 1915, 1922
Stef. Skouloudis 1915-1916
Nikol. Kalogeropoulos 1916
Spyr. Lampros 1916-1917
E. Repoulis 1917
I. Tsirimokos 1917
Nikol. Stratos 1922
Pet. Protopapadakis 1922

Nikol. Triantafyllakos 1922
Anast. Charalampis 1922
Sotir. Krokidas 1922
Styl. Gonatas 1922-1924
G. Kafantaris 1924
Alex. Papanastasiou 1924
Themist. Sophoulis 1924, 1945, 1946, 1947, 1949
Andr. Michalakopoulos 1924-1925
Theod. Pangalos 1925
A. Eftaxias 1926
Georg. Kondylis 1926
Panagis Tsaldaris 1932-1933, 1933-1935
Alex. Othonaios 1933
Const. Demertzis 1935-1936
Ioan. Metaxas 1936 (From 8/4/1936 to 1/29/1941 Dictator)
Alex. Korizis 1941
G. Tsolakoglou 1941-1942 (Occupation)
K. Logothetopoulos 1942-1943 (Occupation)
I. Rallis 1943-1945 (Occupation)
Emman. Tsouderos 1941-1944
Sophoklis Venizelos 1944, 1950, 1951
Georg. Papandreou 1944-1945, 1963, 1964
Nikol. Plastiras 1945, 1950
Petros Voulgaris 1945
Archiepiskopos Damaskinos 1945
Panag. Kanellopoulos 1945, 1967
Panag. Poulitsas 1946
Dimitrios Maximos 1947
Konst. Tsaldaris 1947
Alex. Diomidis 1949
A. Kyriakos1949-1950
Ioannis Theotokis 1950
Dim. Kiousopoulos 1952
Alex. Papagos 1952-1955
Const. Karamanlis 1955-1961, 1974-1980
K. Georgakopoulos 1958
Konst. Dovas 1961
Panag. Pipinelis 1963
Styl. Mavromihalis 1963
Io. Paraskevopoulos 1963-1964, 1966
Georg. Novas 1965
Ilias Tsirimikos 1965
Stef. Stefanopoulos 1965-1966

K. Kollias 1967
G. Papadopoulos 1967-1973 (Dictator)
S. Markezinis 1973
A. Androutsopoulos 1973-1974
Georg. Rallis 1980-1981
Andreas Papandreou 1981-1987, 1993-1996

Source: Data from Epameinondas K. Stasinipoulos (1985). *Kommata Kai Ekloges Sten Hellada: 1821-1985* (7). Athens: Epameinondas K. Stasinopoulos; Enoses Teos Voulefton (1985). *150 Chronia Democratias* (219-220). Athens: Hellenoekdotike.

Tzannetakis 1989
I. Grivas 1989
Xenophon Zolotas 1989-1990
Constantine Mitsotakis 1990-1993
Costas Simitis 1996-Present

Presidents of the Republic
P. Kountouriotis 1924-1926, 1926-1929
T. Pangalos 1926 (Dictator)
A. Zaimis 1929-1935
G. Papadopoulos 1973 (Dictator)
Phaidon Ghizikis 1973-1974 (During Dictatorship)
M. Stasinopoulos 1974-1975
K. Tsatsos 1975-1980
K. Karamanlis 1980-1985, 1990-1995
Christos Sastzetakis 1985-1990
K. Stefanopoulos 1995-Present

Source: Data from Enoses Teos Voulefton (1985). *150 Chronia Hellinikes Democratias* (p. 221). Athens: Helloekdotike.

Kings of Greece
Othon I 1833-1862
George I 1864-1913
Constantine I 1913-1917, 1920-1922
Alexander I 1917-1920
George II 1922-1923, 1935-1947
Paul I 1947-1964
Constantine II 1964-1973

Source: Data from Enoses Teos Voulefton (1985). *150 Chronia Hellenikes Democratias* (p. 221). Athens: Helloekdotike.

Dictators
Th. Pangalos 1926
I. Metaxas 1936-1941
G. Papadopoulos

Source: Data from Enoses Teos Voulefton (1985). *150 Chronia Hellenikes Democratias* (p. 221). Athens: Helloekdotike.

5. According to R. Dunphy (1995): "Democracy can be consolidated only through a number of processes. The powers and role of the state must be delineated, allowing an autonomous civil society to flourish. The new constitution must be accepted by a majority of citizens and political actors. The different interests and views in the society must be effectively represented by parties, which are autonomous from the state and accountable to citizens. Governments must be formed on the basis of a majority, and power must alternate peacefully between government and opposition. The party system must be stabilized and antidemocratic parties must become marginal, preferably through the lack of support. The armed forces must be subordinated to the democratic civilian authorities. Channels of communication and negotiation must be established between the state, parties, and major interest groups. A civic culture must be established in which the concept of citizenship rights and obligations is accepted and understood" (p. 137).

A similar but more precise definition of democratic consolidation is offered by Diamantouros (1984) who states that consolidation "refers to that phase in a new regime's life which is concerned more directly with the erection of that set of institutions and with the institutionalization of that set of formal and quasi-formal arrangements and practices which are likely to maximize the chances of its persistence and smooth operation, thereby further strengthening its legitimacy, and minimizing the probability of regression, of breakdown and of a relapse to non-competitive politics" (p. 51).

6. Larry Diamond (1996) defines civil society as "the realm of organized social life that is voluntary, self-generating, (largely) self-supporting, autonomous from the state, and bound by a legal order or set of set rules" (p. 228).

7. The beginning of the Europeanization process can be traced beck to 1975 when the government submitted its application for Greece to become a full institutional member of the European Community. Greece had been an associate member since 1961. The Europeanization process can be divided into two phases: the first phase began with the fall of the military dictatorship and ended in 1985 with the expiration of the transitional arrangements laid down in the Act of the Accession; the second phase began with the end of the process in which the political implications of joining the European Community and Greece's role in its development gained wider acceptance. During the first phase, the Europeanization process affected domestic developments (contributed to the

consolidation of democracy, compelled administrative adjustments to comply with European Community requirements, and influenced Greece's foreign policy) and simultaneously there was resistance to this process among certain circles. During the second phase many constituencies, including PASOK, changed their position toward Europeanization. The second phase was marked by the decision to seek a loan from the European Community, which subjected Greece to integration requirements and to European Community logic (Ioakimidis, 1996, pp. 35-40).

References

Nicos Alivizatos (1990). "The difficulties of 'rationalization' in a polarized political system: the Greek Chamber of Deputies." In Ulrike Liebert & Maurizio Cotta (Eds.), *Parliament and Democratic Consolidation in Southern Europe: Greece, Italy, Portugal, Spain and Turkey* (131-153). London and New York: Pinter Publishers.

Nicos Alivizatos (1995). "The Executive in the Post-Liberation Period, 1944-1949." In John O. Iatrides & Linda Wrigley (Eds.), *Greece At The Crossroads: The Civil War and Its Legacy*. University Park, PA: The Pennsylvania State University.

G. Anastasiades (1993). *Synchrone Politike Historia Tes Helladas (1974-1992)*. Thessaloniki: Malliaris-Paideia A.E.

G.R. Andrews & H. Chapman (1995). "The Social Construction of Democracy, 1870-1990: An Introduction." In G.R. Andrews & H. Chapman (Eds.), *The Social Construction of Democracy, 1870-1990* (1-28). New York: New York University Press.

Athenian' (1972). *Inside the Colonels' Greece*. London: Chatto & Windus.

Athens News Agency Bulletin (10 April 2000, pp. 1-10). Distributed by the Press Office of the Embassy of Greece in Washington, D.C.

Athens News Agency Bulletin (30 November 2001, pp. 1-6). Distributed by the Press Office of the Embassy of Greece in Washington, D.C.

Athens News Agency Bulletin (5 December 2001, pp. 1-13). Distributed by the Press Office of the Embassy of Greece in Washington, D.C.

Athens News Agency Bulletin (2 January 2002, pp. 1-9). Distributed by the Press Office of the Embassy of Greece in Washington, D.C.

Athens News Agency Bulletin (9 January 2002, pp. 1-12). Distributed by the Press Office of the Embassy of Greece in Washington, D.C.

Athens News Agency Bulletin (29 January 2002, pp. 1-15). Distributed by the Press Office of the Embassy of Greece in Washington, D.C.

Athens News Agency Bulletin (7 January 2002, pp. 1-7). Distributed by the Press Office of the Embassy of Greece in Washington, D.C.

Heinz-Jurgen Axt (1997). "Introduction." In Heinz-Jurgen Axt (Ed.), *Greece and the European Union: Stranger among Partners?* (9-21). Nomos Verlagsgesellschaft: Baden-Baden.

L. Baerentzen & David H. Close (1993). "The British Defeat of EAM, 1944-5." In David H. Close (Ed.), *The Greek Civil War, 1943-1950* (72-96). London & New York: Routledge.

K. Bakatselos (1989). *E Ideologia Tes Apates: Poios dietheiren poion...* Athens: Roes A.E.

Ivo Banac (1995). "The Tito-Stalin Split and the Greek Civil War." In John O. Iatrides & Linda Wrigley (Eds.), *Greece At The Crossroads: The Civil War and Its Legacy*. University Park, PA: The Pennsylvania State University.

John Baylis & Steve Smith (1997). *The Globalization of World Politics: An Introduction to International Relations*. New York: Oxford University Press.

D. Benetatos (1977). *Giati Den Egine Demokratia*. Athens: Ekdoseis "Dodone."

Nancy Bermeo (1995). "Classification and Consolidation: Some Lessons from the Greek Dictatorship." *Political Science Quarterly*, 110, (3), pp. 435-452.

A. Blais & S. Dion (1990). "Electoral Systems and the Consolidation of New Democracies." In D. Ethier (Ed.), *Democratic Transition and Consolidation in Southern Europe, Latin America and Southeast Asia* (250-265). London: Macmillan Press LTD.

Andrew Borowiec (1983). *The Mediterranean Feud*. New York: Praeger.

Davis Brewer (2001). *The Greek War of Independence: The Struggle for Freedom from Ottoman Oppression and the Birth of the Modern Greek Nation*. Woodstock & New York: The Overlook Press.

J.F. Brown (1992). *Nationalism, Democracy, And Security In The Balkans*. Brookfield, USA: Dartmouth Publishing Company.

John Campbell & Philip Sherrard (1968). *Modern Greece*. New York, Washington: Frederick A. Praeger, Publishers.

John K. Campbell (1983). "Traditional Values and Continuities in Greek Society." In Richard Clogg (Ed.), *Greece In The !980s* (184-207). London: McMillan Press LTD.

D. Chondrokoukes (1974). *O Golgothas Tes Hellinikes Demokratias*. Athens: Boukoumanes.

Christian Science Monitor, *The,* 1 August 1964.

Jane Perry Clark Carey & Andrew Galbraith Carey (1968). *The Web of Modern Greek Politics*. New York & London: Columbia University Press.

Myrtle A. Cline (1930). *American Attitude Toward The Greek War Of Independence, 1821-1828*. Atlanta, Georgia: Higgins-McArthur Company.

Richard Clogg (1976). "E Ideologia 'Tes Epanastases Tes 21 Apriliou 1967'." In G. Yiannopoulos & Richard Clogg (Eds.), *E Hellada Kato Apo Stratiotiko Zygo* (81-112). Athens: Ekdoseis Papazese.

Richard Clogg (1987). *Parties and Elections in Greece*. London: C. Hurst & Company.

Richard Clogg (1992). *A Concise History of Greece*. Cambridge, England: Cambridge University Press.

Richard Clogg (1993). "Introduction: The PASOK Phenomenon." In Richard Clogg (Ed.), *Greece, 1981-89: The Populist Decade* (viii-xiv). New York: St. Martin's Press.

David H. Close (1993). "The Reconstruction of a Right-Wing State." In David H. Close (Ed.), *The Greek Civil War, 1943-1950* (156-189). London & New York: Rutledge.

David H. Close (1995). *The Origins Of The Greek Civil War*. London & New York: Longman.

Theodore A. Couloumbis (1975). *Provlemata Hellenoamerikanikon Scheseon*. Athens:

Theodore A. Couloumbis, John A Petropoulos & Harry J. Psomides (1976). *Foreign Interference In Greek Politics: An Historical Perspective*. New York: Pella Publishing Company.

Theodore A. Couloumbis (1978). *Provlemata Hellenoamericanikon Skeseon*. Athens: I.D. Kollarou & Sias A.E.

Theodore A. Couloumbis (1992). "Andreas Papandreou: The Style And Substance Of Leadership." In T.C. Kariotis (Ed.), *The Socialist Experiment: Papandreou's Greece 1981-1989* (85-95). New York: Pella Publishing Company, Inc.

Theodore A. Couloumbis (1993). "Greek-US Relations in the 1990s: Back into the Future." In H.J. Psomiades and S.B. Thomadakis (Eds.), *Greece, The New Europe, and The Changing International Order* (360-395). New York: Pella Publishing Company Inc.

Theodore Couloumbis & P. Yannas (1996). "Greek foreign policy priorities for the 1990s." In K. Featherstone & K. Ifantis (Eds.), *Greece In A Changing Europe: Between European integration and Balkan disintegration* (160-175). Manchester & New York: Manchester University Press.

C.W. Crawley (1973). *The Question of Greek Independence: A Study of British Policy in the Near East, 1821-1833*. New York: Howard Fertig.

D. Dakin (1972). *The Unification of Greece: 1770-1923*. London: Ernest Benn Limited.

A. Danopoulos & L. Gerston (Summer 1990). "Democratic Currents in Authoritarian Seas: The Military in Greece." *Armed Forces and Society*, 16 (4), 529-545.

John G. Demetrokalles (1996). *Aihmalote Demokratia*. Athens: Ekdoseis Papazese.

P.E. Demetras (1991). *Politikos Perigyros, Kommata kai Ekloges sten Hellada*. Vol. II. Athens: Lychnos.

Nikiforos Diamantouros (1984). "Transition to, and Consolidation of, Democratic Politics in Greece: 1974-1983: A Tentative Assessment." In G. Pridham (Ed.), *The New Mediterranean Democracies: Regime Transition In Spain, Greece And Portugal* (50-71). London: Frank Cass & Co. Ltd.

Nikiforos Diamantouros (1991). "PASOK And State-Society Relations In Post-Authoritarian Greece (1974-1988." In Spyros Vryonis (Ed.), *Greece on the Road to Democracy: From the Junta to PASOK* (15-35). New Rochelle, New York: Aristide D. Caratzas.

Nikiforos Diamantouros (1997). "Greek Politics & Society in the 1990s." In Graham T. Allison & Kalypso Nicolaidis (Eds.), *The Greek Paradox: Promise vs. Performance* (23-37). Cambridge, Massachusetts & London: England: The MIT Press.

Larry Diamond (1996). "Toward Democratic Consolidation." In Larry Diamond & M.F. Plattner (Eds.), *The Global Resurgence of Democracy* (227-240). Baltimore & London: The Johns Hopkins University Press.

K. Digaves (1975). *To Emerologio Tes Hountikes Eptaetias*. Thessaloniki: Konstantinos Digaves.

J.P.D. Dunbabin (1994). *The Cold War: The Great Powers And Their Allies*. London & New York: Longman.

Richard Dunphy (1995). "Escaping from the jackboots: Spain, Portugal, Greece." In David Gowland, Basil O'Neil & Alex Reid (Eds.), *The European Mosaic: Contemporary Politics, Economics and Culture* (127-145). New York: Longman.

Economist, The (22 May 1993, 17)

Economist, The (11 September 1993, 53).

Economist, The (9 October 1993, 59-60)

Economist, The (16 October 1993, 57-58)

Economist, The (6 November 1993, 67-68)

Economist, The (25 March 1995, 60)

Economist, The (25 November 1995, 49-50)

Economist, The (27 January 1996, 44-45)

Economist, The (25 February 1996, 53-57)

Economist, The (22 June 1996, 50-51)

Economist, The (14 September 1996, 50-51)

Economist, The (28 September 1996, 60)

Economist, The (1 May 1999, 52)

Economist, The (29 March 1997, 59-60)

Economist, The (1 April 2000, 50)

Richard Ernsberger & Toula Vlahou (21 January 2002). "Greek Revival." In *Newsweek International.*

Europe (February 1996, 8-9)

Europe (October 1997, 14-15)

Kevin Featherstone (1996). "Introduction." In Kevin Featherstone & Kostas Ifantis (Eds.), *Greece In A Changing Europe: Between European integration and Balkan disintegration?* (3-16). Manchester & New York: Manchester University Press.

Earl .H. Fry & Gregory .A. Raymond (1983). "The Adriatic Region: The Politics of Clientilism." In Earl H. Fry, Gregory A. Raymond, David Bohn & James L. Waite (Eds.), *The Other Western Europe: A Political Analysis of the Smaller Democracies* (51-93). Santa Barbara, California & Oxford, England: ABC-Clio Information Services.

M. Goldbloom (1976). "E Politike Ton EPA Ste Petapolemike Hellada." In G. Yiannopoulos & Richard Clogg (Eds.), *E Hellada Kato Apo Stratiotiko Zygo* (345-384). Athens: Ekdoseis Papazese.

Martin E. Goldstein (1984). *America's Foreign Policy: Drift or Decision.* Wilmington, Delaware: SR Scholarly Resources Inc.

S. Gregoriades (1975). *Historia Tes Synchronou Hellados: 1941-1974, Demiourgia kai Politike*. Vol. 4. Athens: K. Kapopoulos.

S. Gregoriades (1975)., *Historia Tes Synchronou Hellados: 1941-1974, E Dictatoria*. Vol. 5. Athens: K. Kapopoulos.

S. Gregoriades (1975). *Historia Tes Synchronou Hellados: 1941-1974, E Dictatoria*. Vol. 6. Athens: K. Kapopoulos.

S. Gregoriades (1975). *Historia Tes Synchronou Hellados: 1941-1974, E Dictatoria*. Vol. 7. Athens: K. Kapopoulos.

R. Gunther, H.J. Puhle & Nikiforos P. Diamantouros (1995). "Introduction." In R. Gunther, H.J. Puhle & Nikiforos P. Diamantouros (Eds.), *The Politics of Democratic Consolidation: Southern Europe in Comparative Perspective* (1-32). Baltimore & New York: The Johns Hopkins University Press.

S. Hadjiyannis (1990). "Democratization and the Greek State." In R.H. Chilcote, S. Hadjiyannis, F.A. Lopez III, D. Nataf & E. Sammis (Eds.), *Transitions from Dictatorship to Democracy* (131-187). New York: Crane Russak.

W.A. Heurtley, H.C. Darby, C.W. Crawley & C.M. Woodhouse (1965). *A Short History of Greece: From Early Times to 1964*. New York: Cambridge University Press.

Steven W. Hook & John Spanier (2000). *American Foreign Policy Since World War II*. Washington, D.C.: CQ Press.

Lynn Hunt, Thomas R. Martin, Barbara H. Rosenwein, R. Po-Chia Hsia, & Bonnie G. Smith (2001). *The Making of the West: Peoples and Cultures*. Boston & New York: Bedford/St. Martin's.

Sammuel P. Huntington (1996). "Democracy's Third Wave." In L. Diamond & M.F. Plattner (Eds.), *The Global Resurgence of Democracy* (3-25). Baltimore & London: The Johns Hopkins University Press.

John O. Iatrides (1995). "Greece at the Crossoads, 1944-1950." In John O Iatrides & Linda Wrigley (Eds.), *Greece At The Crossroads:The Civil War and Its Legacy*. University Park, PA: The Pennsylvania State University Press.

John O. Iatrides & Nicholas X. Rizopoulos (Spring 2000). "The International Dimension of the Greek Civil War." *World Policy Journal*, Vol. XVII, No. 1, 87-103.

K. Ifantis (1996). "Greece and the USA after the Cold War." In K. Featherstone & K. Ifantis (Eds.), *Greece In A Changing Europe: Between European integration and Balkan disintegration* (147-159). Manchester & New York: Manchester University Press.

P.C. Ioakimidis (1984). "Greece: From Military Dictatorship To Socialism." In A. Williams (Ed.), *Southern Europe Transformed: Political and economic change in Greece, Italy, Portugal and Spain* (40-69). London: Harper and Row, Publishers.

P.C. Ioakimidis (1996). "Contradictions between policy and performance." In Kevin Featherstone & Kostas Ifantis (Eds.), *Greece In A Changing Europe: Between European integration and Balkan disintegration* (33-52). Manchester & New York: Manchester University Press.

P.C. Ioakimidis (1998). *Europaike Henose Kai Helliniko Kratos*. Athens: Themelio.

Barbara Jelavich (1987). "Tsarist Russia and Greek Independence." In John T.A. Koumoulides (Ed.), *Greek Connections: Essays on Culture and Diplomacy*. Notre Dame, Indiana: University of Notre Dame Press.

Charles Jelavich & Barbara Jelavich (1965). *The Balkans*. Englewood Cliffs, New Jersey: Prentice-Hall.

Donald Kagan, Steven Ozment & Frank M. Turner (1995). *The Western Heritage*. Englewood Cliffs, New Jersey: Prentice Hall.

George Stergiou Kaloudis (1991). *The Role of the U.N. in Cyprus from 1964 to 1979*. New York: Peter Lang.

G. Karagiorgas (1975). *Apo ton IDEA ste Hounta*. Athens: Ekdoseis Papazese.

T.C. Kariotis (1992). "The Rise And Fall Of The Green Sun." In T.C. Kariotis (Ed.), *The Greek Socialist Experiment: Papandreou's Greece 1981-1989* (11-33). New York: Pella Publishing Company.

Pavlos Karolides (1992). *Istoria Tou Hellinikou Ethnous*. Athens: Ekdoseis Kaktos.

E. Kartakis (1993). *O Karamanlis tes Metapolitevsis: Oi megales paremvaseis 1974-1992*. Aigaleo, Greece: POES A.E.

J. Katres (1974). *E Gennese Tou Neophasismou Sten Hellada*. Athens: Ekdoseis Papazese.

D.K. Katsoudas (1991). "New Democracy: In Or Out Of Social Democracy?" In Spyros Vryonis, Jr. (Ed.), *Greece on the Road to democracy: From the Junta to PASOK 1974-1986* (1-14). New Rochelle, New York: Aristide D. Caratzas.

Keesing's 14 no. 2 (5-12 September 1964): 20269.

Charles W. Kegley & Gregory A. Raymond (2002). *Exorcising the Ghost of Westphalia: Building World Order in the New Millennium*. Upper Saddle River, New Jersey: Prentice Hall.

Dimitris Kerides (1997). "Greece in the 1990s: The Challenge of Reform." In Graham T. Allison & Kalypso Nicolaidis (Eds.), *The Greek Paradox: Promise vs. Performance*. Cambridge, Massachusetts & London, England: The MIT Press.

F. Kleanthis (1983). *Etsi Hasame Ti Mikra Asia*. Athens: I.D. Kollarou & Sias A.E.

J.V. Kofas (1989). *Intervention and Underdevelopment: Greece During the Cold War*. University Park & London: The Pennsylvania State University Press.

John S. Koliopoulos (1977). *Greece and the British Connection: 1935-1941*. Oxford: Oxford University Press.

Y.A. Kourvetaris & B.A. Dobratz (1987). *A Profile of Modern Greece In Search Of Identity*. Oxford: Clarendon Press.

George A. Kourvetaris (1999). *Studies on Modern Greek Society and Politics*. New York: Columbia University Press.

George D. Kousoulas (1965). *Revolution and Defeat: The Story of the Greek Communist Party*. London: Oxford University Press.

George D. Kousoulas (1973). *Greece: Uncertain Democracy*. Washington, D.C.: Public Affairs Press.

George D. Kousoulas (1974). *Modern Greece: Profile of a Nation*. New York: Charles Scribner's Sons.

Stephen D. Krasner (1999). *Sovereignty: Organized Hypocrisy*. Princeton, New Jersey: Princeston University Press.

John Van der Kriste (1994). *Kings of the Hellenes: The Greek Kings, 1863-1974*. Dover, New Hampshire: Alan Sutton Publishing.

M.C. Kurop (January/February 1998). "Greece and Turkey: Can the Mend Fences?" *Foreign Affairs*, 77 (1), 7-13.

Thomas D. Lancaster (1990). "The Politics of Greece." In Roy C. Macridis (Ed.), *Modern Political Systems: Europe* (264-279). Englewood Cliffs, New Jersey: Prentice Hall.

J.E. Lane & S.O. Ersson (1994). *Politics and Society in Western Europe*. London, Thousand Oaks, New Delhi: SAGE Publications.

Keith R. Legg & John M. Roberts (1997). *Modern Greece: A Civilization on the Periphery*. Boulder, Colorado: Westview Press.

Spyros Linardatos (1986). *Apo ton Emphylio ste Hounta*. Athens: Ekdoseis Papazese.

J.J. Linz, A. Stephan & R. Gunther (1995). "Democratic Transition and Consolidation in Southern Europe, with Reflections on Latin America and Eastern Europe." In R. Gunther,

Nikiforos P. Diamantouros & H.J. Puhle (Eds.), *The Politics of Democratic Consolidation: Southern Europe in Comparative Perspective* (77-123). Baltimore & London: The Johns Hopkins University Press.

J.J. Linz & A. Stepan (1996). *Problems of Democratic Transition and Consolidation: Southern Europe, South America, and Post-Communist Europe*. Baltimore & London: The Johns Hopkins University Press.

S.M. Lipset (Spring 1998). Excerpts from "Three Lectures on Democracy." *Extensions*, 4-13.

J.C. Loulis (1984-1985, Winter). "Papandreou's Foreign Policy." Foreign Affairs, 63 (2), 375-391.

J.C. Loulis (1995). *E Ktise Tes Politikes Sten Hellada: Ekloges - Koine Gnome, Politikes Exelixeis, 1980-1995*. Athens: I. Sideres.

B. Lyrintzis (1984). "Political Parties in Post-Junta Greece: A Case of 'Bureaucratic Clientilism'?" In G. Pridham (Ed.), *The New Mediterranean Democracies: Regime Change In Spain, Greece And Portugal* (99-118). London: Frank Cass & Co. Ltd.

C. Lyrintzis (1993). "PASOK in Power: From 'Change' to Disenchantment." In Richard Clogg (Ed.), *Greece, 1981-89: The Populist Decade* (26-46). New York: St. Martin's Press.

Maclean's (29 January 1996, 25)

R. Macridis (1981). "Elections and Political Modernization in Greece." In H.R. Penniman (Ed.), *Greece at the Polls: The National Elections of 1974 and 1977* (1-20). Washington & London: American Enterprise Institute for Public Policy Research.

Roy C. Macridis & Thomas D. Lancaster (1987). "The Politics of Greece." In R.C. Macridis (Ed.), *Modern Political Systems: Europe* (333-346). Englewood Cliffs, New Jersey: Prentice-Hall Inc.

Aristovoulos I. Maneses (1987). *E Exelixe Ton Politikon Thesmon Sten Hellada: Anazetontas Mia Dyskole Nomimopoiese*. Athens: Akdose Ant. N. Sakkoula.

K. Maxwell & S. Spiegel (1994). *The New Spain: From Isolation To Influence*. New York: Council On Foreign Relations Press.

John Mavrogordato (1931). *Modern Greece: A Chronicle And A Survey, 1800-1931*. London: MacMillan And Co., Limited.

George Mavrogordatos (1983a). *Stillborn Republic: Social Coalitions and Party Strategies in Greece, 1922-1936*. Berkley: University of California Press.

George Mavrogordatos (1983b). "The emerging party system." In Richard Clogg (Ed.), *Greece In The 1980s* (70-94). London: McMillan Press LTD.

Mark Mazower (1993). *Inside Hitler's Greece: The Experience of Occupation, 1941-44.* New Heaven & London: Yale University Press.

John P. McKay, Bennett D. Hill & John Buckler (1987). *A History of Western Society*, Vol. II. Boston: Houghton Mifflin Company.

Dennis Merrill & Thomas G. Paterson (Ed.), (2000). *Major Problems in American Foreign Relations, Vol. II: Since 1914.* Boston & New York: Houghton Mifflin Company.

John Merriman (1996). *A History of Modern Europe: From Renaissance to the Present.* New York & London: W.W. Norton & Company.

L. Morlino (1987). "Democratic Establishments: A Dimensional Analysis." In E.A. Baloura (Ed.), *Comparing New Democracies: Transition and Consolidation in Mediterranean Europe and the Southern Cone* (53-78). Boulder & London: Westview Press.

L. Morlino (1995). "Political Parties and Democratic Consolidation in Southern Europe." In R. Gunther, Nikiforos P. Diamantouros & H.J. Puhle (Eds.), *The Politics of Democratic Consolidation: Southern Europe in Comparative Perspective* (315-388). Baltimore & London: The Johns Hopkins University Press.

L. Morlino & J.R. Montero (1995). "Legitimacy and Democracy in Southern Europe." I. R. Gunther, N.P. Diamantouros & H.J. Puhle (Eds.), *The Politics of Democratic Consolidation: Southern Europe in Comparative Perspective* (231-260). Baltimore & London: The Johns Hopkins University Press.

Yannis G. Mourelos (1985). "British Policy Towards King Constantine's Dethronement and Greece's Entry Into The War." In P. Calvocoressi, R. Clogg, D. Dakins, J. Hassiotis, B. Kondis, Y. Mourelos, M. Pearton, N. Petsalis-Diomidis, H. Seton-Watson, C. Svolopoulos, C. Woodhouse (Eds.), *Greece and Great Britain During World War I* (131-138). Thessaloniki:Institute for Balkan Studies.

Nicos Mouzelis (1978). *Modern Greece: Facets of Underdevelopment.* London: The Macmillan Press LTD.

Nicos Mouzelis (1987). *Koinovouleutismos kai Ekviomehanise sten Emi-Peripheria: Hellada, Balkania, Latinike Amerike.* Athens: Themelio.

New Statesman and Society (26 January 1996, 10-11)

E.M. Pantelouris (1987). *Greece: an introduction.* Moffat, Scotland: Solway Offset Services, Ltd., Dumfries.

Victor S. Papacosma (1977). *The Military In Greek Politics: The 1909 Coup D' Etat*. Kent, Ohio: Kent University Press.

Victor S. Papacosma (1983). "The Historical Context." In Richard Clogg (Ed.), *Greece In The 1980s* (30-42). London: McMillan Press LTD.

Andreas G. Papandreou (1974). *E DemoKratia Sto Apospasma*. Athens: Ekdoseis Karanase.

Paul Constantine Pappas (1985). *The United States And The Greek War For Independence, 1821-1828*. New York: Columbia University Press.

Thomas G. Paterson, J. Garry Clifford & Kenneth J. Hagan (2000). *American Foreign Relations: A History Since 1895*. Boston & New York: Houghton Mifflin Company.

J. Pesmazoglou (1976). "E Hellinike Oikonomia Meta To 1967." In G.N. Yiannopoulos and Richard Clogg (Eds.), *E Hellada Kato Apo Stratiotiko Zygo* (136-181). Athens: Ekdoseis Papazese.

J. Petras, E. Raptis & S. Sarafopoulos (1993). "Greek Socialism: The Patrimonial State Revisited." In J. Kurth & J. Petras (Eds.), *Mediterranean Paradoxes: Politics and Social Structure in Southern Europe* (160-224). Oxford: Berg Publishers, Inc.

James Pettifer (1993). *The Greeks: The Land And People Since The War*. New York: Viking.

James Pettifer (1996). "Greek political culture and foreign policy." In Kevin Featherstone & Kostas Ifantis (Eds.), *Greece In A Changing Europe: Between European integration and Balkan disintegration?* (17-23). Manchester & New York: Manchester University Press.

Pontiki, To (1989). *Oi Ekloges Tes 18es Iouniou 89*. Athens: To Pontiki.

Pontiki, To (1990). *Oi Ekloges Tes 5es Noemvriou 89*. Athens: To Pontiki.

Pontiki, To (1990). *Oi Ekloges Tes 8es Apriliou 1990*. Athens: To Pontiki.

Pontiki, To (1994). *Oi Ekloges Tes 10es Octovriou 1993*. Athens: To Pontiki.

N. Poulantzas (1976). *The Crisis of the Dictatorships: Portugal, Greece, Spain*. London: Humanities Press.

G. Pridham (1990). "Political parties, parliaments and democratic consolidation in southern Europe: empirical and theoretical perspectives." In U. Liebert & M. Cotta (Eds.), *Parliament and Democratic Consolidation in Southern Europe: Greece, Italy, Portugal, Spain and Turkey* (225-248). London & New York: Pinter Publishers.

G. Pridham (1995). "The International Context of Democratic Consolidation: Southern Europe in Comparative Perspective." In R. Gunther, N.P. Diamantouros, & H.J. Puhle (Eds.), *The Politics of Democratic Consolidation: Southern Europe in Comparative Perspective* (166-203). Baltimore & London: The Johns Hopkins University Press.

H.J. Psomiades (1982). "Greece: From the Colonels' Rule to Democracy." In J.H. Herz (Ed.), *From Dictatorship To Democracy: Coping with the Legacies of Authoritarianism and Totalitarianism* (251-273). Westport, Connecticut: Greenwood Press.

N. Psyroukis (1983). *Istoria Tes Synchrones Helladas (1967-1974): To kathestos tes 21 Apriliou.* Athens: Epikairoteta O.E.

H. Richter (1980). "The Battle of Athens and the role of the British." In M. Sarafis (Ed.), *Greece: From Resistance to Civil War* (78-90). Nottingham, England: Spokesman.

Bruce Russett & John R. Oneal (2001). *Triangulating Peace: Democracy, Interdependence, and International Organizations*. New York & London: W.W. Norton & Company.

Spyros Sakellaropoulos (1998). *Ta Aitia Tou Aprilianou Praxikopematos*. Athens: "Nea Synora."

P. Schmitter (1991). "An Introduction to Southern European Transitions from Authoritarian Rule: Italy, Greece, Portugal, Spain, and Turkey." In G. O'Donnell, P. Schmitter, and L. Whitehead (Eds.), *Transitions from Authoritarian Rule* (3-10). Baltimore & London: The Johns Hopkins University Press.

P. Schmitter (1996). "Dangers And Dilemmas Of Democracy." In L. Diamond & M.F. Plattner (Eds.), *The Global Resurgence of Democracy* (76-93). Baltimore & London: The Johns Hopkins University Press.

Robert D. Schulzinger (1990). *American Diplomacy In The Twentieth Century*. New York: Oxford University Press, Inc.

P. Schwab & G.D. Frangos (1970). *Greece Under The Junta*. New York: Facts on File, Inc.

G. Smith (1986). *Politics In Western Europe: A Comparative Analysis*. Aldershot, England: Gower Publishing Company Limited.

D.A. Sotiropoulos (1996). *Populism and Bureaucracy: The Case of Greece Under PASOK, 1981-1989*. Notre Dame & England: University of Notre Dame Press.

Epameinondas K. Stasinopoulos (1985). *Kommata Kai Ekloges Sten Hellada: 1821-1985*. Athens: Epameinondas K. Stasinopoulos.

Nikolaos A. Stavrou (1999). "The Dismantling of the Balkan Security System: Consequences for Greece, Europe, and NATO." In Nokolaos A. Stavrou (Ed.), *Mediterranean Security at the Crossroads: A Reader* (187-208). Durham, North Carolina: Duke University Press.

L.S. Stavrianos (1952). *Greece: American Dilemma and Opportunity*. Chicago: Henry Regnery Company.

Nikos G. Svoronos (1976). *Episkopese Tes Neoellenikes Istorias*. Athens: Themelio.

Peter J. Stavrakis (1995). "Soviet Policy in Areas of Limited Control: The Case of Greece, 1944-1949." In John O. Iatrides & Linda Wrigley (Eds.), *Greece At The Crossroads: The Civil War and Its Legacy*. University Park, PA: The Pennsylvania State University.

T.G. Tatsios (1984). *The Megali Idea and the Greek-Turkish War of 1897: The Impact of the Cretan Problem on Greek Irredentism, 1866-1897*. New York: Columbia University Press.

Sir James Emerson Tennent (1845). *History of Modern Greece, from its Conquest by the Romans B.C. 146, to the Present Time*. London: Henry Colburn, Publisher.

Stavros B. Thomadakis (1995). "The Greek Economy and European Integration: Prospects for Development and Threats of Underdevelopment." In Dimitri Constas & Theofanis G. Stavrou (Eds.), *Greece Prepares for the Twenty-first Century* (101-123). Baltimore & London: The Johns Hopkins University Press.

P. Tourkovasilis-Galanos (1980). *Ta Politika Kommata Meta to 1967*. Athens: Ekdoseis Papazese.

US News & World Report (14 January, 1991), 41.

A. Vakalopoulos (1987). *Nea Hellenike Historia*. Thessaloniki: Ekdoseis Vanias.

Thanos Veremis (1983). "Security Considerations and Civil-Military Relations in Past-war Greece." In Richard Clogg (Ed.), *Greece In The 1980s* (173-183). London: McMillan Press LTD.

Thanos Veremis (1987). "The Military." In K. Featherstone & D.K. Katsoudas (Eds.), *Political Change In Greece Before And After The Colonels* (214-229). London & Sydney: Croom Helm.

Thanos Veremis (1992). *Hellada-Europe: Apo Ton Proto Polemo Os Ton Psychro Polemo*. Athens: Plethron.

Thanos Veremis (1997). *The Military in Greek Politics: From Independence to Democracy*. Montreal, New York, London: Black Rose Books.

I. Vergopoulos (1990). "The Political Economy of Democratic Consolidation in Southern Europe." In D. Ethier (Ed.), *Democratic Transition and Consolidation in Southern Europe, Latin America and Southeast Asia* (139-154). London: The Macmillan Press LTD.

S. Verney (1987). "Greece And The European Community." In K. Featherstone & D.K. Kastoudas (Eds.), *Political Change In Greece Before and After The Colonels* (253-270). London & Sydney: Croom Helm.

S. Verney & Theodore A. Couloumbis (1991). "State-international systems interaction and the Greek transition to democracy in the mid-1970s." In G. Pridham (Ed.), *Encouraging Democracy: The International Context of Regime Transition in Southern Europe* (103-124). Leicester, London: Leicester University Press.

S. Verney (1996). "The Greek Socialists." In J. Gaffney (Ed.), *Political Parties and the European Union* (170-188). London & New York: Routledge.

Enoses Teos Voulefton (1985). *150 Chronia Hellenikes Democratias*. Athens: Hellenoekdotike.

J. Wilkinson & H.S. Hughes (1998). *Contemporary Europe: A History*. Upper Saddle River, New Jersey: Prentice Hall.

C.M. Woodhouse (1968). *A Short History of Modern Greece*. New York, Washington: Frederick A. Praeger, Publishers.

C.M. Woodhouse (1976). "E 'Epanastase' Sto Historiko Tes Plaisio." In G.N. Yiannopoulos and Richard Clogg (Eds.), *E Hellada Kato Apo Stratiotiko Zygo* (3-55). Athens: Ekdoseis Papazese.

C.M. Woodhouse (1985). *The Rise and Fall of the Greek Colonels*. London, Toronto, Sydney, New York: Granada Publishing.

C.M. Woodhouse (1991). *Modern Greece: A Short History*. London: faber & faber.

G.N. Yiannopoulos (1976). "Oi Antistasiakes Dynameis Meta To Praxikopema." In G.N. Yiannopoulos & Richard Clogg (Eds.), *E Hellada Kato Apo Stratiotiko Zygo* (256-291). Athens: Ekdoseis Papazese.

G. Zacharopoulos (1976). "E Politike Kai O Stratos Ste Metapolemike Hellada." In G.N. Yiannopoulos & Richard Clogg (Eds.), *E Hellada Kato Apo Stratiotiko Zygo* (56-80). Athens: Ekdoseis Papazese.

S. Zormpalas (1978). *O Neophasismos Sten Ellada (1967-74)*. Athens: "Synchrone Epoche."

Index

Note: Unless otherwise noted, all entries refer to events and conditions in Greece. Additionally, unless otherwise noted, all personal titles are attributable to Greece.

About the Author

Dr. George Stergiou Kaloudis is a Professor of Government at Rivier College, Nashua, New Hampshire.